Praise for *Mark Twain, the World, and Me*

"In Mark Twain, the World, and Me, Susan Harris shows great skill in describing both the pull and the personal stakes that brought her into such a sustained, fruitful engagement with Mark Twain—a cultural icon who seems to radiate 'unlikeness' with regard to her own roots and upbringing. There's no self-indulgence here; instead, we see the high-risk adventure that informs the best literary scholarship."
—Bruce Michelson, author of *Printer's Devil: Mark Twain and the American Publishing Revolution*

"This enormously compelling memoir of Harris's attempt to retrace Twain's travels during his 1895–1986 round-the-world lecture tour is more than simply an engaging work of creative nonfiction, it might just be the best book-length work of scholarship yet written on Twain's Following the Equator."
—Joseph Csicsila, coauthor of *Heretical Fictions: Religion in the Literature of Mark Twain*

"Writing with great a understanding and appreciation of Twain, Harris shows how the issues that engaged him in his travels still invite discussion today. This insightful book opens a window on a person, and a past, that continues to resonate."
—*Publishers Weekly*

"In this engaging memoir, Susan Kumin Harris tracks Mark Twain around the globe, reflecting upon her own story and identity to provide new insight into Twain's fascinating and contradictory mind. As a Jewish woman married to an African American man, Harris is uniquely positioned to reconsider the modern relevance of Twain's writings on religion, the fluidity of race and gender, and more as she retraces his journeys from Australia to India to South Africa. It's a trip worth taking."
—Andrew Beahrs, author of *Twain's Feast: Searching for America's Lost Foods in the Footsteps of Samuel Clemens*

Susan K. Harris is distinguished professor emerita at the University of Kansas. She is author of *God's Arbiters: Americans and the Philippines, 1898–1902*; *The Cultural Work of the Late Nineteenth Century Hostess: Annie Adams Fields and Mary Gladstone Drew*; *The Courtship of Olivia Langdon and Mark Twain*; *19th-Century American Women's Novels: Interpretive Strategies*; and *Mark Twain's Escape from Time: A Study of Patterns and Images*.

MARK TWAIN, THE WORLD, AND ME

Mark Twain, the World, and Me

Following the Equator,
Then and Now

SUSAN K. HARRIS

THE UNIVERSITY OF ALABAMA PRESS

Tuscaloosa

The University of Alabama Press
Tuscaloosa, Alabama 35487-0380
uapress.ua.edu

Inquiries about reproducing material from this work should
be addressed to the University of Alabama Press.

Typeface: Scala Pro and Didot

Cover image: Portrait of Samuel L. Clemens with top hat and
umbrella, London, England; courtesy of the Mark Twain Project, The Bancroft Library, University of California, Berkeley
Cover design: David Nees

Cataloging-in-Publication data is available from the Library of Congress.
ISBN: 978-0-8173-5967-6
E-ISBN: 978-0-8173-9283-3

An early version of chapter 2, "Pollution," was first published under the title
"Mother Ganga" in *Catamaran Literary Reader* 3, no. 4 (Winter 2015): 53–62.
A version of chapter 1, "Pilgrimage," was published under the title "My Life with
Mark Twain: Chapter One—Hinduism" in *The Mark Twain Annual* 15 (2017): 1–21.

Contents

Illustrations

Acknowledgments

A project as far-flung as this one incurs many debts, not least to the people willing to talk, advise, and guide me. My first thanks go to my colleagues at the University of Kansas (KU), who encouraged my travels and were generous with contacts, especially Lorraine Haricombe, then-dean of the KU Libraries; Professors Hannah Britton (political science and women's studies); Tailan Chi (international business); Ebenezer Obadare (sociology); Surendra Bhana (history, emeritus); Byron Caminero-Santangelo (English); and Anna Neill, then-chair of the English department. Colleague Stephanie Fitzgerald, professor of English and Indigenous studies, gave me a crash course (and reading list) in Aboriginal and Māori history over lunch, which was essential for getting me started. Thank you, Stephanie. I am also indebted to the Hall family, whose funding of my distinguished professorship enabled the travel, and to Victor Bailey, professor of history and then-director of the Hall Center for the Humanities, whose wise guidance of the institute made it a world-class center for the exchange of ideas. If I have omitted any other colleagues, my sincere apologies.

Once on the road my contacts were extraordinary. In Australia I especially thank Rob Pascoe (professor of history at Melbourne's Victoria University) and Susan Pascoe (then-director of the Australian Charities and Not-for-Profits Commission) for their warmth, hospitality, generosity, and above all, friendship; Peter Dann, research manager at Phillip Island Nature Parks; Andrea James, playwright and artistic director of the Melbourne Workers Theatre; Maryrose Casey, professor with the Monash Indigenous Studies Centre, Monash University, Melbourne; and Cathy Craigie, former executive director of the First Nations Australia Writers Network. I also profited greatly from talks with Paul Giles and Judith Barbour, both of the English Department at the University of Sydney; with Don Watson, writer; and with Robin Annear, librarian and local historian in Castlemaine. In a crunch moment I texted the Mark Twain Papers at Berkeley asking for information, and editor Leslie Myrick fired back just what I needed—thank you! In New Zealand I am especially indebted to Maureen Montgomery, lecturer at New Zealand's University of Canterbury; and to Alex and Sarah Calder, professors at the University of Auckland and the University of Otago, respectively. In India, my warm thanks to Seema Sharma, professor at the University of Mumbai, an informant who has become a good friend. My husband and I had fewer "personal" contacts in India than in other countries, but we had some exceptionally good guides and drivers, among them, in Mumbai, guide Lakshmi and driver Anise—of Anise my journal reads: "I really like Anise. He is a good person. And one hell of a driver. I should have been scared, but I wasn't." Delhi introduced us to guide Jimmy and driver Baldev; the latter drove us around the "Golden Triangle" and proved one of the most interesting people we met in India. Jaipur featured guide Asoke Kumar Sharma, who worked exceptionally hard to teach us the history of his city and region, and in Varanasi we were indebted to Manish Develi, who skillfully plotted our learning curve. Guide Deep took us through modern-day India in Kolkata. To these and other guides, drivers, cooks, and helpers, we extend our warm thanks.

South Africa, too, proved a wonderful source of generous people willing to talk, inform, guide, and even entertain us. Among these I especially thank Harold Herman, dean emeritus of the faculty of education, and Stan Ridge, emeritus professor of English, both at the University of the Western Cape; Diana Ferrus, poet; Willie Bester, artist; and Paul and Doreen Abelman. From Howard College, University of KwaZulu-Natal (Durban), I thank Professors Lindy Steibel, Margaret Daymond, and Betty Govinden, of the English Department; Johann Wassermann, professor of education history, and Saleem Washington, professor of music. In Johannesburg and Pretoria, warm thanks to Nithaya and Anashree Chetty, who invited us into their home, to Alice Brown—human rights advocate and independent consultant at Sojourner, Tubman, Wells and Co. Consulting—who offered us the viewpoint of an African American living in South Africa; and to Isabel Hofmeyr, professor of African literature at the University of Witwatersrand and global distinguished professor at New York University. Isabel has offered us not only time, advice, and support but also friendship, which we value deeply.

Back home I received constant support from friends and colleagues during the entire process of writing, revising, and publishing this book. My warmest thanks to friends who read and commented on sections: Rufus and Anne Hallmark, professors emeritus at Rutgers University and the New England Conservatory, respectively; Pam McCarthy, deputy editor, *The New Yorker*; Deb Clarke, vice provost and professor of English, Arizona State University; Linda Morris, professor emerita, Department of English, University of California, Davis; Chad Roman, then-editor of *The Mark Twain Annual*, and Catherine Segurson, editor in chief of the *Catamaran Literary Reader*. Thanks also to the librarians and staff of the many libraries I have used, especially those at the University of Kansas, Cornell University, and the New York Public Library Berg Collection. A special acknowledgement for Pat Crain, professor of English at NYU, who sponsored me for a library pass there. Over the years Elmira College's Center for Mark Twain Studies, under the successive administrations of Gretchen Sharlow, Barbara Snedecor, and Joe Lemak, has granted me numerous summer weeks in residence at its scholars' retreat at Quarry Farm, where Twain wrote many of his best-known works. Thank you— for your support, for maintaining the Farm's library of primary and secondary resources, and for the opportunity to experience one of Twain's own favorite places. And huge thanks as always to the wonderful editors at the Mark Twain Project at the University of California, Berkeley, especially general editor Bob Hirst, who answered *all* my many emails almost as fast as I wrote them! Thanks too to the Mark Twain Foundation for its efficient and generous handling of all Twain copyright issues.

My writing group has been a source of constant support: deep thanks to Paul Lauter, professor of English, Trinity College, emeritus; and to Erica Burleigh and Bettina Carbonell, both professors of English at the John Jay College of Criminal Justice, City University of New York. At the University of Alabama Press, my sincere thanks to Dan Waterman, editor in chief; to the anonymous readers who approved the manuscript; to Kristen Hop, acquisitions editor; and to the entire production team at the press for their assistance in bringing this book into existence. And a last minute shout-out again to Rob Pascoe, who stayed with us in Brooklyn just before the manuscript was due into press and copyedited all eight chapters in the interstices of a conference he was attending. I can't imagine a more generous gift. Thank you, Rob!

First and last, though, my deep gratitude to Billy, who has as always been my friend, lover, confidence booster, reader, adviser, and companion. Thank you, thank you, for agreeing to be my travel partner through these adventures. They would not have been the same without you!

MARK TWAIN, THE WORLD, AND ME

Me, World, Twain

An Introduction

I wasn't wild about visiting Australia. It had never been on my personal
bucket list, not the way the Galápagos Islands are, or the grasslands
of Central Asia. I didn't think I could stand the long flight, for starters.
I'm mildly claustrophobic and a bad sitter, and the prospect of all those
hours in a plane made me queasy. I also was never grabbed by the *idea*
of Australia, which seemed too much like the United States to be worth
the effort. But I was following Mark Twain on his 1895–1896 lecture tour
around the world, and he spent two months Down Under, so I tamped
down my anxieties and flew. Australia was the first stop on a research
project that I spread out over fifteen months: a month in Australasia,
another in India, a third in South Africa. I started with a list of Twain
related sites to visit and archives to explore—a routine academic research
itinerary. I managed to visit about half of the sites, but I barely set foot in
the archives. The project morphed almost as soon as my plane touched
down in Sydney.

It started as a cartographical realignment, a radical shift in my sense
of place. I knew, intellectually, that Australia was somewhere below
Southeast Asia, but in my head North America is the center of the world
map, and Australia is in the lower left-hand corner. My trip had begun
from the Kansas City airport, the hub closest to Lawrence, Kansas, where
I lived and taught at the University of Kansas. From there I flew to Hous-
ton, Texas, and then straight to Australia—a nineteen-hour flight. Not
only was I phenomenally jet-lagged, but for my first couple of days in
Sydney my brain assumed that I was in the United States looking over at
myself perched on that lower-left corner. I didn't start to *feel* like I was in
Australia until—go on, laugh—I was sitting in the Sydney Opera House
watching a production of *South Pacific*. (I know, I know—it's ridiculous
to go to Australia to see *South Pacific*, especially since it was a production
I'd seen before and hadn't particularly liked, but that's what was playing,
and I wanted to see the Sydney Opera House.) I'm happy to report that
the cast was far better than the one at Lincoln Center, but the significant
moment came with the staging. A huge, World War II map of the South
Pacific functioned as the backdrop for most of the scenes. It had seemed
academic when I saw it in New York, but this time I thought, "Wow!
I'm *in* the South Pacific," and suddenly my geographical orientation

reconfigured itself, like when you twist a kaleidoscope and all the colored pieces tumble around and end up in a different pattern.

My research agenda saw a similar shift. Suddenly library research looked tiresome. I didn't want to spend my three weeks in musty archives. I was in Australia; I wanted learn about the country, not about a few individuals' conversations with an American visitor over a hundred years ago. I didn't have to drop Twain to change my focus; instead I reoriented the project, just as my Opera House moment had reoriented my sense of place. Instead of reading Australians' comments about Mark Twain, I would begin with Twain's comments about Australians and take my thematic cues from there. Twain traipsed through Fiji, Australia, New Zealand, India, Mauritius, and South Africa observing and commenting, and I could learn about contemporary Australia (and later, about New Zealand, India, and South Africa) by testing those comments in light of today. For instance, he insisted that in all his trips through the Australian countryside, he never saw a kangaroo, and that he had to visit a zoo to see native Australian fauna. That's one comment I followed up; a journey into wildlife preservation that took me from Sydney zoos to South African wildlife refuges and back to the little penguin colony outside Melbourne. Suddenly, the kinds of research I was doing shifted from the purely academic, from fleshing out already well-developed stories about Mark Twain, to a much wider, more comprehensive set of questions about the myriad ways that human beings around the world are grappling with pressing problems like wildlife conservation, pollution, religious difference, and racial and gender categorization.

The new framing excited me because it called on far more of my interests than a historically defined authorial study would allow. It also brought me into the project, as a character in my own right. The personal is pretty much verboten in academic writing, so this was a whole new playing field for me. It meant figuring out my relationship to the material in a way I'd never ventured before, including digging into personal memory to understand why I come at things the way I do. I've always lived a kind of dual life. My first eighteen years were divided between home and abroad, between growing up as a middle-class Jewish kid in Baltimore, Maryland, and family sojourns, from two to fourteen months each, in the countries where my peripatetic father worked: Puerto Rico, Colombia, Nepal, Switzerland. The conflicts arose after we came home. I'd missed my Baltimore kid-life intensely, but each time I returned it was a little harder to reintegrate into my friends' cozy existence. I'd seen a bigger world than the other girls' narrow round of school, B'nai B'rith

Girls, hairstyles, TV, and movies. Most of my friends couldn't take a bus downtown without a parent along; I flew alone to India the summer I turned thirteen. My friends didn't want to hear about my travels, so I pretended they hadn't happened. As long as our chatter focused on hairstyles and math homework, no problem.

The uneasiness came with social issues, particularly civil rights. Late 1950s Baltimore was being desegregated, against its will. My grade school had been integrated during the year I spent in Bogotá, Colombia, and local white mothers warned us that the junior high school was full of "Negroes with knives." No one in my family bought into the white paranoia, but it gives you an idea of the environment my brothers and I had to negotiate. I was a preadolescent, already too fat and from too weird a family to blend in easily. To complicate matters, my travels had taught me some very alien (to Baltimore) ideas about the value of racial and cultural diversity. I cringed when my B'nai B'rith chapter chanted "two, four, six, eight / we don't want to integrate" as our bus drove through a black neighborhood. In retrospect I realize the incident accelerated my moral development, because the shame I felt at that moment propelled me out of that crowd. As I got older I drifted farther and farther away from Baltimore's insular Jewish community, drawn to companions who could share at least some of my values, if not my experiences. That didn't mean I forsook Judaism, only that I searched for Jews who, like me, were eager to explore and embrace the world. It also didn't erase my sense of marginality—by high school I was the Jew among Christians, the white among Negroes, and still, the traveler among entrenched locals. The quality of my friends rose, but my position remained tangential to the mainstream. College didn't help matters; four years at Antioch, an institution long dedicated to producing graduates imbued with social justice ideals, plus a year at Oxford's working-class Ruskin College, brought me to a point where I had very little in common with Baltimore. My 1968 marriage to an African American finalized the separation.

So there I was in Sydney in 2013, chasing a writer who in many ways epitomized the white, Christian, American mainstream of the late nineteenth century, and who, even when he rejected that community's values, still depended on them for his living. Economic power demands subservience (I'd learned that lesson early, in fights with my father), and Mark Twain often played to his audience's worldview. At the same time, he also often spoke out against the racism, bigotry, and political expediency that ruled the United States throughout the late nineteenth century, and he railed against European states that were raping and pillaging their way to domination in Africa, Asia, and the Middle East. I'd always sensed that Twain and I shared an edgy, marginal relationship to our contemporaries—especially when we perceived our compatriots refusing others the rights and opportunities they enjoyed themselves. With this, I admired Twain because he wasn't afraid to change his mind. Over his lifetime he struggled with his culturally inherited racism, sexism, and sense of white Western superiority, and by the 1890s—the decade on which I'm focusing here—he had rethought many, though certainly not all, of his earlier assumptions. Part of my pleasure in studying his works came from watching him evolve. In many ways that's what brought me to this project; in 2011 I had published a book (*God's Arbiters: Americans and the Philippines*) focused on his resistance to the US annexation of the Philippines in 1899, and I wanted to figure out how he got there. My hunch was that the trip around the world had taught him the perils of colonialism, so I was going to try to find out more about his experiences in the British colonies he visited. That turned out to be a lot harder than it originally appeared because *Following the Equator*, the book he wrote about the lecture tour, gyrates between celebrating and criticizing the British colonial presence. Even though I think I understand Twain's fluctuations, the inconsistencies of this book continue to baffle me.

Baffle, yes, but not put off. It's that sense of dual positioning that draws me, that experience of marginality we share. Like me, Samuel Clemens was both of and not of his community. Despite being a white, male, Protestant Christian from a respectable if cash-poor middle-class American family, he was also a midwesterner in Eastern high society, a school dropout among the highly educated, an admirer of Chinese culture in a time of virulent anti-Chinese sentiment, a sympathizer with African Americans during the nadir of American race relations, and an outspoken critic of US foreign policy at a time when doing so invited charges of treason. His ability to make people laugh leavened his critical commentary, but it didn't make him any less marginal to the mainstream, which alternated between celebrating him when he supported their positions and trashing him when he didn't. It took me years to figure out that the mainstream academy's insistence that Twain was not a "serious" writer was its own variation on this form of social bullying. Translation of "not serious": Twain spoke to ordinary people, he engaged politically, he challenged received wisdoms, he was really funny, and his humor could make people squirm.

Being marginal means that you are always thinking outside your companions' boxes, bringing in information they reject, configuring the world differently from their patterns. Sometimes you are with them, in lockstep; just as often you find yourself saying "but." It means you suck at mass exercises like standardized exams, because you are always thinking about exceptions, about other ways of doing things. Your inability to wholeheartedly embrace any one worldview keeps you roaming, searching for a resting place. The upside is a very broad perspective, stretching across multiple sets of colleagues, friends, and ideological communities. The downside is that there is no social or intellectual space that is quite "home." And you are, rightly, open to accusations of inconsistency. Inconsistencies are the result of your thinking across—and responding to—more than one worldview at a time.

So there we were in Australia, Mark Twain and I, both of us carrying the weight of our long histories (Twain was sixty when he began his around-the-world tour; I was sixty-eight when I began following him), our unorthodox ways of thinking, and our sense that, straddling old and new centuries as we both did, we were riding waves of tumultuous change across the globe. Twain was naturally curious, which is one of the traits I like most about him, and his curiosity about his new environment created my new agenda and the new agenda dictated very different research patterns than I normally use, so I decided to copy Twain's—sort of. Twain was actually a good researcher. Compared to mine, his resources were limited, but he did well with what he had, studying artifacts, reading accounts of encounters between settlers and natives, and pumping his British hosts. He collected guidebooks, histories, missionary accounts, and newspapers as he moved, but he had time to read seriously only when he was on ships, traveling between continents. While he was on tour, he relied on local informants to explain what he was seeing. His informants were almost entirely English or the descendants of English settlers—the inheritors of the Empire's self-justifications. By the 1890s self-justifying narratives were ubiquitous; over the centuries of British rule the Empire's administrators had developed a series of plot outlines that made them the heroes of their own stories and pushed the native communities they were supplanting to (you got it) the margins. So much though by no means all of Twain's information came from sources inherently biased against the people they were usurping.

Marginal people tend to notice other marginals. In Australia, Twain was curious about the Aborigines. They caught his attention because they were so marginal that he never even met one. Killing Aborigines had been a blood sport among the settlers of an earlier generation, and some of the tales Twain heard about the massacre of whole communities appalled him. Though the killing was no longer (officially) condoned, the white power structure was still doing its damnedest to relegate Australia's First Peoples to the continent's past. Ethnography, then a new science, was complicit. In the late nineteenth century ethnography focused on material objects, and the British construction of Aboriginal ethnography rested on examples of their arts and technologies, which the British enthusiastically collected and around which they wove narratives justifying white rule. Aborigines were "savages," the story went, and as such were incapable of adjusting to the modern world. Therefore they should be allowed to die off—with a little help from their white friends. In its gentler version this is an Aussie version of the "disappearing Indian" narrative of the United States; in its nastier version it was a prescription for slow genocide.

That's how Twain came into contact with Aborigines—through their objects and the stories the British wove around them. Twain examined the artifacts carefully, impressed by technologies like the boomerang and the weet-weet (also known as the woomera) and rating their pictorial art as equal to the lower rungs of "civilized" art (FE 218).[1] But he was also baffled by the Aborigines' apparent indifference to material culture, their disdain for housing, clothing, "stuff." Western civilization was predicated on just such "stuff," and that was the only criterion Twain and his hosts knew for judging whether a culture was civilized. The Aborigines didn't make it, and yet, as we'll see, Twain wasn't entirely comfortable with this assessment.

I started with artifacts, too. I figured ethnographic museums would give me an overview, a way into this new culture, so my first morning in Sydney I made my way to the Australian Museum, which was supposed to have a good Aboriginal and Torres Strait Peoples collection.[2] I didn't much look forward to this phase of my research. I've never been engaged by Native American exhibits, and I didn't expect to be engaged by Aboriginal ones. But this exhibit drew me right in. In retrospect I realize I'd been put off by the American museums' presentations, not the collections themselves. My posttravel research into museology (a new word for me) has taught me that Native American exhibits in major US museums tend to be controlled by white curators, which means that they rarely reflect Indians' own voices and points of view. A 2015 article by Sheila Regan on the "Plains Indians" exhibit in the new Native American wing of Kansas City's Nelson-Atkins Museum of Art—an exhibit I'd seen with the same sense of disappointment I'd always felt in Native American exhibits—quoted Deanna Dart, one of the few Native American curators, who contends that in most American museums "Indians are a thing of the past. If they don't still practice the culture, they're not still Indians" (3). The article confirmed my own experiences. I was accustomed to being presented with an object—usually something no longer used, like a warbonnet or saddlebag—informed of its name and function, and, in best-case scenarios, provided with a short, dispassionate explanation of the object's significance in its time. But that's it. The displays left me with little sense of the past and no sense whatever of the present, of what makes Native American communities special, what they care about, how they live, love, grieve. Their cultures are presented piecemeal, a collection of objects with no human glue.

In contrast, Aboriginal voices sound through Australia's major museums. Not only do the communities' passions resonate across the museum labels, but many of the exhibits feature videos in which individual Aborigines discuss their sense of place in family, clan, and nation. Australia's Aboriginal exhibits threw me into twenty-first-century Indigenous Australian culture, offering me Indigenous voices, allowing me to hear them speak. That's a truly major difference, both between my former museum experiences and this one and between my own experiences and Twain's. Aborigines were presented to Twain as the past, a disappearing race leaving little or no cultural residue. Indigenous Australians were presented to me as the present, a present intimately connected to its past and fighting for its future. I heard Indigenous voices in exhibit labels, I saw Indigenous Australians in supermarkets and on the street, I talked to Indigenous curators and to Indigenous writers in coffee shops. I saw movies made by Indigenous filmmakers and read books written by Indigenous writers. Like Twain, I pumped the locals, and I collected lists of books and articles to be read and internet sites to investigate after I got home. Libraries are still central to my research. But in putting together this book, I realized that what I bring to my research—my personal and familial background, the varied environments in which I grew up and in which I live now, my academic interests and training, and the events of my own contemporary world—affects my writing as much as Twain's own background, environments, and audiences affected his.

This book, then, is the story of my adventures following Mark Twain on his 1895–1896 lecture tour through the British Empire. It is also the story of my relationship with Mark Twain, an Author (capital "A") who died thirty-five years before I was born. Twain's travelogue of his journey, *Following the Equator*, both compels and repels me, emotions elicited by the confluences and clashes of Samuel Clemens's values and my own.[3] In

Figure 1. On board the *Flyer* between Tacoma and Seattle, start of the around-the-world tour, 1895. Photograph by James B. Pond; courtesy of the Mark Twain Project, Bancroft Library, University of California, Berkeley.

bringing myself into the story I'm forced to confront those values, which often means digging deeply into my own personal history to see how I came to where I am. It also means asking myself what it means to be following an Author, and who this "I" is, in relation to both that Author and my own past. The dynamic between Twain and Me is one of this book's central themes. But the essays presented here are also stories about "the

World"—its present and its past, starting with Mark Twain's observations about the Australia, India, and South Africa he visited in 1895–1896 and then moving to those countries as I encountered them 115 years later.[4] Twain traveled with his wife, Livy, and daughter Clara; I traveled with my husband, Billy (a.k.a. William J. Harris, himself a scholar of twentieth-century American literature). Though only occasionally figuring directly into our texts, accompanying "family" contextualized both Twain's journey and my own, accounting for the "we" running through both our books and affecting our perceptions of the dynamics of our encounters. The essays come at those dynamics from many angles, from funeral rites to religion, conservation to biraciality. This book is many stories intertwined, taking us from the then to the now, taking me from myself to Twain and back again, and taking us all into some of the legacies of Twain's world as they exist in our time.

Mark Twain's 1895 – 1896 Lecture Tour Around the World

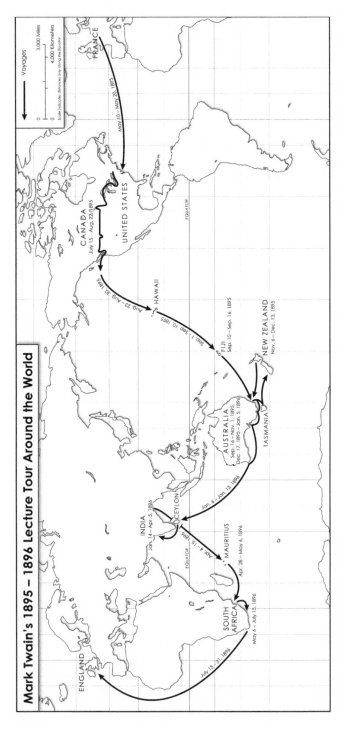

Source: Adapted with permission from R. Kent Rasmussen, *Critical Companion to Mark Twain: A Literary Reference to His Life and Work.*, New York: Facts on File, 2007, 127.

I

Pilgrimage

When I was eight years old I ran with a gang of Jewish kids who lived in my garden apartment complex in Baltimore. A tiny Orthodox synagogue—a remnant from the past—stood behind the buildings, and the only people who ever came there were old men wrapped in prayer shawls. We liked them because they let us drink the shabbos wine, so we used to come to shul on Friday nights to get drunk. We'd play around while the old men swayed and chanted, biding our time until they invited us up to the bimah and poured out the wine. I don't think my mother ever knew.

That was in 1953. Fast-forward sixty years and I'm watching the Aarti ceremony at the Dashashwamedh Ghat in Varanasi, India, and my brain is flipping up memories of the old men in the shul. It must have been the chanting that triggered them, along with the bowing and bending of the priests and their assistants, and the constant shifting of the crowd. The Aarti is a fire-offering ritual, performed every evening at dusk on the Dashashwamedh Ghat—one of Varanasi's many flights of steps and platforms (ghats) leading down from the city to the Ganges River. It features multiple priests, golden candelabras, conch blowing, bell ringing, and loud, rhythmic chanting. It was way noisier and more spectacular than our old men's shabbos prayers, but there was something about it that felt familiar. When I mentioned the sensation to my cousin Rebecca, she reminded me that Judaism is an oriental religion. I'd never really thought of it that way—to me Judaism's always just been Baltimore.

Being Jewish was the last thing I expected to think about when I set off to follow Mark Twain around the world. Jews don't figure much in *Following the Equator*, and I didn't plan on visiting any Jewish sites. Yet my sense of myself as a Jew turned out to be one of the identities I brought with me on my journeys, along with being American, white, and female. All four were highlighted as I moved through the spaces Twain visited. They were points of vulnerability and of insight, places where I felt either endangered or empowered. My religious background in particular, both my grounding in Jewish identity and my familiarity with other religions throughout my life, contrasted sharply with Twain's own religious experiences. Twain's Presbyterian upbringing, his antipathy to Roman Catholicism, and his discomfort with any religion that he had been taught to regard as "idolatrous" placed him squarely in the Protestant mainstream of nineteenth-century America, whereas my own history stimulated my interest in the many ways that human beings understand their relationship to the divine. The contrast helped me understand why Twain came at India the way he did. My personal identities were also the flip side of my neutral professorial persona, which was how I usually presented myself: "Good morning! I'm a Mark Twain scholar, and I'm researching Twain's trip around the world. May I look at your archives?"

I think the Jewishness came up because so much of Twain's commentary is about religion, especially in India. Twain called India "a country of a thousand religions and two million gods," and it is still a place where religion lives and breathes. You sense it in the crowds going in and out of the temples and mosques, and in the freshness of the offerings in the omnipresent street-side shrines. I liked it. But the noisy rituals that I found oddly comforting, Twain found incomprehensible and irrational. Measuring the distance between our responses to Indian religions, Hinduism especially, forced me to confront some of the differences between me and the man whose life and work has been my major topic of study for most of my professional life. Despite both being Americans, we brought very different personal experiences and cultural narratives with us, which meant that when we encountered the new and strange, we processed it along very different routes. We also had recourse to vastly different kinds of resources. Twain took notes during his travels, then plunked himself down in London to write *Following the Equator*. Extant letters from him show that he consulted numerous books as he wrote, some of which he asked Chatto and Windus, his English publisher, to buy for him. Others he took out from a branch of the London library.[1] I followed the same path (modernized), taking sketchy notes and photos on my cell phone during the day, then uploading pictures to the cloud and expanding my notes on my iPad at night. After I got home, I too plunked myself in the library for some hard research. My resources are far better than Twain's, of course—I have the advantage of academic libraries, more than one hundred years of additional events, and a variety of research skills, not to speak of the internet. On the other hand, Twain wasn't hampered by the mandate for objectivity with which my academic training nags me, so he could go through documents until he found what he wanted, then plug it into his narrative framework.

Which brings me to our differing goals and audiences. The reason

Figure 3. Aarti ceremony, Dashashwamedh Ghat, Varanasi, India, 2008; photograph by Yusuke Kawasaki. https://www.flickr.com/photos/u-suke/3156784664/ CC BY 2.0.

Twain embarked on the lecture tour around the world was that he had been forced to declare bankruptcy, and he desperately needed *Following the Equator* to sell.[2] That meant he was willing to write to his audience's expectations, one of which was that Indians were irrational and their religion impenetrable. As I noted earlier, I originally undertook this project because I wanted to understand the origins of Twain's later anti-imperialism, and I thought that the trip around the world might explain it. My project has shifted, and I'm still trying to figure out my audience, but I suspect it will have minimal overlap with Twain's. Finally, we are very different people, beginning with gender, century, religion, and social strata, and we view the world from radically different perspectives. There are places in *Following the Equator* that upset and anger me, places where Twain attacks rather than explores the cultures he visits, places where he bares his prejudices in ways that I wish he wouldn't. In trying to understand what he didn't get, and why, I've found my sense of my relationship to Twain shifting from detached, scholarly "objectivity" to my own personal and cultural history, and to the ways that our very different histories nevertheless define us both as Americans. Religion, a flash point in our country since its founding, is one of those areas.

Twain spent two months in India, crisscrossing the country by train or cruising the coasts by ship. He also spent a lot of that time in hotel rooms, plagued by bronchitis, carbuncles, and diarrhea. When he wasn't traveling or confined to his room, he lectured, partied, and toured, attending dinners in both British and Indian homes and visiting the sites the British designated as of interest to foreigners. These included religious sites—the Empire's administrators needed to understand Indian religious practices in order to conduct business with their colonial subjects. An apparatus for indoctrinating tourists was well established—by 1896 the British had been in India for close to three hundred years, ample time to create a system of multilingual native guides and to encourage the production of guidebooks telling visitors what they should see, and why. By the end of the nineteenth century they had also developed a series of cultural narratives that "interpreted" India to the West. Although many of the narratives have been challenged since Independence (1947), they still rule most visitors' perceptions. And because they are rooted in strongly held Western concepts of self and world, it is very hard to get around them, especially regarding religion.

To some extent Twain did try to understand India's religions, especially toward the beginning of his sojourn there. In Bombay (now Mumbai) he observed, as closely as permitted (meaning he stood outside, at a respectful distance), the Parsi Temples of Silence on Malabar Hill, where the dead are taken to be exposed to the weather and to the vultures that devour the corpses' flesh, leaving only clean bones to be disposed of. Indian Parsees are descendants of Iranian Zoroastrians, whose faith holds that corpses are impure and should not be permitted to pollute any of the four elements: earth, air, fire, or water. Twain grasped the Parsi focus on purity behind the practice, but his free associations led him away from comparative religions rather than toward them. He moved from comparing Parsi rituals to funeral practices in America and the growing acceptance of cremation there, to comparing the swift cleanliness of fire and the slow moldering of bodies in the grave. It's not that he was disrespectful of Parsi practices; it's that his stream of consciousness worked through his own cultural experience—the nascent turn to cremation in the West and his own dread of corporal disintegration.

Twain's next set of comments about the Parsees shows us the power of the British narratives through which he understood what he saw in India. One of the puzzles of the India portion of *Following the Equator* is Twain's sudden shift in attitude toward the British Empire. Twain had visited Australia and New Zealand (both still British colonies) before he landed in India, and genocide, including cultural genocide, is a running theme in the book. His critique of white settlers picks up after the India section as well; his final stop on the tour was South Africa, where he comments (briefly) on the prevailing racism against black Africans. In contrast, he seems absolutely gung ho about British control over India— an embrace of Empire that baffles modern Western readers and infuriates most Indians. But this is where the cultural narratives kick in, a fusion of Twain's own American experiences and ongoing British justifications for England's control over India. As I read through histories of the British in India, I began to see how, brief as the Parsi section is in *Following*, Twain's musing is a perfect example of the confluence of personal and cultural narratives. It's also one of the sections where I find myself dragged into them whether I want to be or not.

The British liked the Parsees—they saw Parsi values and talents as much like their own, and they were happy to train young Parsi men to take positions in the colonial government. They also admired the community's mercantile bent—their ability and willingness to participate in the Empire's trade. Hence Twain's summary in *Following*: "The Parsees are a remarkable community. There are only about 60,000 in Bombay . . . but they make up in importance what they lack in numbers. They are highly educated, energetic, enterprising, progressive, rich, and the Jew himself is not more lavish or catholic in his charities and benevolences. The Parsees build and endow hospitals, for both men and animals; and they and their womenkind keep an open purse for all great and good objects. They are a political force, and a valued support to the government. They have a pure and lofty religion, and they preserve it in its integrity and order their lives by it" (*FE* 378).

The reference to the Jews jars me every time—there I am, called out on a page that seemingly has nothing to do with me. It seems arbitrary, rhetorical, but the fact that Twain compared Parsees to Jews tells us a lot about him as a white Protestant American—and the fact that his words jar me tells me a lot about my own insecurity as a Jewish American. Twain's words reflect one of the cultural narratives through which Western Christians had long viewed the cultural minority in their midst: "the Jew," the narrative maintains, is inherently mercantile, a talent at once enviable and despicable. Liberal Christians leavened the portrait by recognizing the Jewish community's emphasis on charity and civic responsibility. That doesn't mean they were particularly comfortable with us or cared to mix with us socially, only that they had constructed a viable means of imagining—and doing business with—a religious minority that had long lived among them. Twain's comparison reminds me that my sense of comfort in US society was hard-won by my grandparents, most of whom were just arriving in the United States at the time Twain was visiting India. My parents and grandparents were familiar with the restrictive environment the narrative facilitated—nominally, Jews in America were free to do whatever they wanted; in actuality their presence was highly restricted and they were subject to overt acts of exclusion and Jew baiting. Born in the post-Nazi era when anti-Semitism had become politically incorrect, I rarely experienced overt hostility, but I do remember my childhood shock when I learned that Jews were "restricted" on Maryland's Eastern Shore— meaning we could drive through but could not stay at the hotels or stop at the beaches. Twain's casual reference to Jews reminds me that my sense of security in my American identity is always contingent on the moment's cultural tide, and that the fact of my Jewishness can come up even in situations that have absolutely nothing to do with me. I've always known in the back of my mind that Samuel Clemens would consider me an outsider, but I usually suppress the knowledge. Until I hit a comment like this one, which brings it all out in the open.

But, getting away from my personal angst (one reason academics write in the third person), Twain's comparison of Parsees and Jews as mercantile communities also suggests that the "minority-immigrant-community-as-rich-and-powerful-traders" narrative wasn't exclusive to the United States, or even to Jews alone. It was, and remains, a Western construct applied globally. I've heard it used to identify the role of the Chinese in South Asia (often described as "the Jews of Asia"), and clearly the British engaged it to explain the Parsees in Hindu India. Although the Parsees had been in India for a millennium, the British regarded them as different from the Hindus, whom they distrusted. According to the British, the Parsi community was solid, sober, and charitable; most importantly, their religion didn't prevent them from doing business with the Empire or administering colonial rule. Already familiar with the narrative in his own environment, Twain understood Bombay's Parsees through its structure.

Twain also visited a Jain temple in Bombay. In *Following the Equator* Twain confesses that he cannot remember the details of the visit, only that their Indian guide spoke to them in "masterly English." Other than that, Twain reports, "I have nothing left of that episode but an impression: a dim idea of a religious belief clothed in subtle intellectual forms, lofty and clean, barren of fleshly grossnesses; and with this another dim impression which connects that intellectual system somehow with that crude image, that inadequate idol—how, I do not know" (*FE* 379).

We don't have to rely on Twain's faulty memory in this case. His guide, Sri Virchand Raghavji Gandhi, left his own record of the Clemenses' visit to the temple. It is reprinted as an appendix to Keshav Mutalik's 1978 *Mark Twain in India*. The "inadequate idol" to which Twain refers in *Following* was one of the stone images lining the temple's walls. For the Protestant Clemenses, stone images equaled idols, and Livy and Clara joined Twain in asking how Jains understood the images. Trying to bridge the conceptual gap between Eastern and Western religious representations, Gandhi replied that the images represented prophets, not gods, and he compared them to American "demigods" like George Washington or Abraham Lincoln. Gandhi had visited the United States as a representative to the Congress of Religions (part of the 1893 Chicago World's Fair), and he had clearly grasped the quasi sainthood with which Americans had imbued their "Founding Fathers." What he didn't grasp was that even though he could see that his hosts had deified their political forefathers, Americans themselves wouldn't describe the process in quite that way. Hence comparing the images Twain was seeing to statues of Washington or Jefferson was, for Twain, misleading. The images were in fact of Tirthankaras, the pure souls who, Hinduwebsite. com informs us, appear periodically throughout human history, serving as reminders of the path humans must follow to achieve spiritual liberation. They are in a way "Founders," but they are symbols, not deities— far more "holy" than a US Founding Father, but still not divine. Twain wanted to make sure he understood: "The images themselves, then, are not the gods," Gandhi quotes him as saying. Gandhi does not record his own reply.

The family then questioned their guide as to the differences between religions in India. Livy asked how Jainism, Brahminism (by which she may have meant Hinduism), and Buddhism differed (short answer: Jainism predates and highly influences many strains of both Hinduism and Buddhism); Clara wanted to know how worship was conducted. Gandhi told them about Yakshas, beings who, though mortal, live on a different plane of life from ordinary humans, and about some of the differences denoted by the marks on various visitors' foreheads. He also explained the significance of the Jain swastika, the four arms of which represent the four stages of life.

Twain tries to understand the concept of nirvana, and he asks Gandhi whether the prophets—the Tirthankaras—had entered nirvana. When Gandhi affirms that they had, Twain interprets the concept as a state of "perfect rest." Gandhi agrees. "And it must therefore," adds Twain, "be a state of unconsciousness." "No," Gandhi corrects him, "it is a state of perfect consciousness which is keen at all times." Twain doesn't understand: "How can that be?" he asks.

Gandhi's reply begins in a conceptual arena that would have been familiar to the Clemenses—basic Lockean psychology. In our ordinary state, he reminds his guests, we rely on our sense organs for information from the outer world, which we then convert into knowledge. But according to the Jains, this knowledge is imperfect: "The spirit," Gandhi explains, "is covered over by a veil which does not allow full knowledge to enter in. If by some process, the veil can be removed forever, the spirit can know everything without passing through the processes of sensation and perception. We claim that these prophets have reached that state and live in a pure perfected spiritual condition—they have entered the Kingdom of Heaven."

"'I had a different idea of Nirvana,' observed M.T. 'I thought it was all unconsciousness. Now it gives me a different idea'" (Mutalik 106–11).

Twain may have consciously forgotten the details of this conversation, but I think it entered into his unconscious, to be reborn—and transformed—in the solipsistic manuscript fragment that now concludes William Gibson's edition of No. 44, The Mysterious Stranger, where, in a bitter Twainian twist, the idea of "perfect consciousness," indestructible and untrammeled by the flesh, appears not as rest but as torture. I'll be revisiting this passage later, when I talk about Twain and dreaming; for now the incident's significance lies in Twain's comment that he couldn't reconcile Jainism's "lofty," "intellectual" metaphysics with the "crude images" that lined the walls. The idols—for that was how Twain saw them—were the problem. In the end, stone images, in combination with the structure of Hindu rituals and priestly functions, stood in the way of Twain's ability to grasp Hinduism's concepts. His blindness is revealed in almost all the sections he wrote about Benares, the city where, as he noted, religion is the main order of business.

Benares (now Varanasi) was, and remains, the consummate Hindu holy city.[3] It is situated on the Ganges River, and Mother Ganga, as the faithful know the waterway, is at the heart of Hindu cosmology. Mother Ganga is always pure, and she purifies; hence pilgrims flock to bathe in her waters. The city itself is the center from which all else was created, and it is also a *tirtha*, a crossing-over place, where virtuous souls can, on dying, cross directly to nirvana, thus circumventing the cycle of reincarnation. Consequently Benares is a place where pious Hindus come to die, and cremation is a major business on the ghats along the waterfront.

I loved Varanasi. Because Billy and I were staying in the cantonment, the old British section of town several miles from the city center, on the first evening of our stay Manish, our guide, took us by rickshaw—a tuk tuk—into the old city and then walked us through the markets to the Dashashwamedh Ghat, a structure Twain definitely visited. That's where my memories of the old men popped up. We came just as the Aarti ceremony was beginning. This isn't an event Twain would have witnessed, at least not on this ghat; the Aarti has been performed there only since the late 1990s. For me it was a transformative experience. I felt the magic as soon as we arrived at the top of the stairs, mainly because of the river, which spreads out flat, wide, and majestic at this point. It was dusk, and miniature boats holding prayer fires floated on the water alongside orange chrysanthemum garlands offered to Mother Ganga. The view is best from the Shiva temple perched above the ghat, so we clambered up. Below us, the faithful crowded the steps. They also arrived by water, filling the graceful old rowboats that nosed up to the riverside platforms where the ceremony was performed. There five priests, dressed in red and gold and each on his separate platform, performed the rites. Tiered candelabras, all golden, were the centerpiece of each platform—with their candles all lit, the priests raised and lowered them, while bells rang furiously and loudspeakers broadcast the chanting and singing. It was noisy and mesmerizing. I shot a short video of it on my cell phone; looking at it brings back my sense, very intense while I was there, that this ritual had a real relationship to the old men in the shul.

Twain would not have had that memory or found a sense of connection. He would have found the ceremony chaotic, as he found the rest of

Benares. It's not that he didn't like the city—quite the contrary. "Benares was not a disappointment," Twain notes (*FE* 479), and he inscribed
a line that is quoted in almost every book or article about the city that I
have read: "Benares is older than history, older than tradition, older even
than legend, and looks twice as old as all of them put together" (*FE* 480).
Benares is an ideal place for an inquisitive Westerner to seek information about Hindu faith and practice, and guides these days are prepared
to teach religious fundamentals. My journal reminds me that Manish
began our education in Hinduism, Buddhism, and Varanasi history in
the car, right after picking us up from the airport. By the time we got to
the hotel, he had gone through reincarnation and the major gods, and he
continued lecturing throughout the Aarti ceremony. Not only that; over
the next few days he plotted our learning curve for both Hinduism and
Buddhism. For instance, our day in Sarnath, the Varanasi suburb where
the Buddha came to preach after his enlightenment, began with visits to
four Buddhist temples, each built by a different nationality (and therefore
each having a different, often political, "take" on religion), and then to
the archaeological museum. Manish reasoned that we would appreciate
the art objects much more if we knew the stories behind them. He was
right. We came away from Varanasi with at least a sketchy idea of the
Hindu pantheon, a smattering of Hindu cosmology and metaphysics, a
sense of the Buddha's presence in Sarnath, a rich appreciation for the
artifacts in the museum, and a desire to return to Varanasi to explore
further, and more deeply.

Varanasi wasn't just an education in comparative religions, though.
It was also a place where I reconnected to fragments of my own religious
history. The memories that started flipping up weren't only about being
Jewish in Baltimore. Another set was about the summer of 1958, which I
spent in Kathmandu, Nepal. My father was working there, and my older
brother Gerson, who had accompanied Dad, was at St. Xavier's, a Jesuit
boarding school outside of town. Dad was then working for the International Labour Organization, an offshoot of the original League of Nations.
ILO policy included paying for dependents to visit parents during summer holidays (I suspect this policy went back to the days when British
civil servants stationed in India routinely packed their children off to
British boarding schools during the school year). When I found out that
the ILO would pay my fare, I persuaded my mother to let me fly over to
visit Dad and Gerson for two months. I liked it so much that at the end
of the summer I begged to be allowed to stay. I'd made friends with the
daughter of an Indian Airlines pilot whose family roomed in the same

palace that we did. During the winter she attended boarding school in the foothills, and I wanted to go there, too. Dad refused; I suspect he thought looking after one American kid in a Nepalese boarding school was enough. So at the end of the summer—on my thirteenth birthday—I reluctantly flew home.

Not, however, before I'd had a good dose of the sights, smells, and sounds of Hinduism and Buddhism. Nepal is 80 percent Hindu, and its landscape is dotted by temples (many now destroyed in the earthquake of 2015). Buddhism is the second-largest religion, and its presence, too, is very strong. Wherever I went, I was surrounded by the sounds of chanting and the scent of incense. On weekends we went walking in the area that is now Godavari National Botanical Gardens, and I watched the pious wash themselves in the row of stone faucets—the "Five Taps"— at the Hindu temple complexes nearby. I also learned to turn the Buddhist prayer scrolls at Boudhanath and Swayambhunath Stupas, sending prayers to heaven. Back in town, just off one of the many temple squares, there was a house said to be home to the Kumari, a goddess, then a little girl of about seven. I glimpsed her only once, but her story fascinated me. I wondered what it would be like to be "discovered" as a goddess, taken out of my natal family (no biggie; at thirteen, I didn't much like mine anyway), and raised in seclusion as someone set apart from the ordinary. I both pitied and envied her.

All of which is to say that for me in 2013, Varanasi opened the fonts of memory, casting up moments when I had connected to religious ritual in the past and creating a sense of comfort in, and adult curiosity about, the Hinduism and Buddhism that I was reencountering. That was not Twain's experience. Although he toured many temples and museums, floated down the Ganges, and visited the major ghats, Twain took an increasingly hostile attitude toward the religious objects and rituals he observed. Despite his earlier display of interest in Jainism and Zoroastrianism, in Benares he refused to even try to understand Hinduism. Instead, he filtered everything he saw through his always-latent anticlericalism and his general suspicion of institutional religion.

When I compare Twain's and my own responses to Varanasi, I realize that in addition to personal histories, guides had a lot to do with both. Twain had British functionaries and the occasional Indian intellectual like Sri Virchand Raghavji Gandhi. Billy and I had Manish: young, informed, conscientious, and a self-identified Brahmin. Era made a big difference too. Mark Twain visited Benares in 1896, near the height of the British Empire. We visited Varanasi in 2013, sixty-six years after

Independence. Perhaps Manish's grandparents remembered the Raj; Manish certainly didn't. Throughout India, our guides spoke variously of the British era—some regarded it favorably, others with hostility (and still others, we learned, adjusted their attitude to the nationality of their clients). Twain's guides were part of the British colonial structure, as were the books he consulted. Partly because of the English guidebook to Benares he used to prod his memory while writing *Following*, and partly because he grew up in the fervently anti-Catholic Midwest, the sight first of material images used as objects of worship, and second of the ubiquity of Brahmin priests, triggered his satirical faculties rather than his intellectually curious ones. The interesting result is that in his Benares chapters we see two hitherto contradictory forces at work in tandem: Twain's own Protestant grounding on the one hand, and his distrust of established religion on the other.

I came to Varanasi as (among other identities) a professional researcher and an American who had lived through, and embraced, the multiculturalism of the previous half century. I also came as a nonpracticing Jew who had grown up surrounded by both practicing Jews and Catholics. Maryland was settled by English Catholics, and the Baltimore of my youth was a Catholic town. I knew a few Protestants, but the people who mattered in my life either davened or crossed themselves. Because Dad worked in the international arena, I also spent a portion of my childhood in Latin America, where the Roman Catholic Church dominated everyday life. I went through a couple of heavy flirtations with Catholicism, especially in adolescence, and I still find Catholic churches a good place to meditate. Catholic rituals, with their own chants and scents, were part of the religious associations I brought to India.

Pretty much the opposite was true for Mark Twain. If the sensory appurtenances of Judaism, Catholicism, Hinduism, and Buddhism were the religious fabric I brought to Varanasi, Samuel Clemens brought precisely the Protestant sensibilities that abhorred them. I see Twain's writings about Benares within three contexts. The first is his anti-Catholicism. Twain may have stereotyped Jews, but he didn't attack us; by Christian standards of the time, he was pretty tolerant. In contrast, he actively attacked the Catholic Church. This came directly out of his own cultural background: reared in a Presbyterian household with a strong Calvinist bent, Sam Clemens also grew up during a virulently anti-Catholic moment in American history, and he imbibed many of its prejudices. However, Twain's animus was against the institutional church, not its adherents. His anti-Catholic sentiments did not prevent him from socializing and working with individual Catholics, and he actively acknowledged them as a sector of the public he sought to reach through his subscription publishing company, Charles Webster and Company. For instance, in 1886 Webster and Company published Fr. Bernard O'Reilly's authorized biography of Pope Leo XIII, a venture that Twain (wrongly) calculated would pay off royally because "every Catholic in Christendom [will] have to buy a copy as a religious duty" (quoted in Gold 107). He also wrote a novel about a devoutly Catholic woman himself: *Personal Recollections of Joan of Arc, by the Sieur Louis de Conte* (1896). Despite these forays into the Catholic world and readership, Twain's distrust of the institutional church runs throughout his writings, for instance in sections of *A Connecticut Yankee in King Arthur's Court* (1889), and even through *Personal Recollections of Joan of Arc*. His attacks on the institution played to Americans' antiestablishment instincts: church power, church doctrine, and the priesthood all function as the villains in his work.

The Catholic Church wasn't Twain's only religious target, however. Twain distrusted established religions generally, and that distrust is the second context he brought to India. Twain's personal struggles with religious belief were complex—scholars argue constantly over whether or not he believed—but it is clear to everyone that Samuel Clemens disliked the cultural power that established religions wielded, and he attacked it whenever he could.[4] "Concentration of power in a political machine is bad," his spokesperson Hank Morgan opines in *A Connecticut Yankee in King Arthur's Court*. "And an Established Church is only a political machine" (*Connecticut Yankee* 161).[5] From this viewpoint, Twain's attacks on the Catholic Church are a subset of his campaign against religious establishments. Morgan supports Protestantism over Catholicism not from intrinsic merit but because he figures that the numerous Protestant sects "will police each other"—a form of free trade in the religious marketplace. When Twain got to Benares, his animus against religious institutions and his distrust of the church joined with British narratives about Hinduism to influence his assessment of the Hindu establishment, especially Brahmin priests.

Twain's third context for his Benares writings is the British colonial environment in which he moved. He was in India primarily to entertain the Empire's employees, and they played host to his entire trip. This included acting as his chief informants: as we have already seen in his report on the Parsees, the story of India Mark Twain imbibed was the Empire's narrative about the vast land and peoples they were seeking to "uplift"—a word frequently used to mask imperialist exploitation.

The Reverend Arthur Parker's 1895 *Guide to Benares*, the text on which Twain relied when describing the city for his readers, was part of this. *Guide to Benares* was the authoritative guidebook for English-speaking visitors to that city at the end of the nineteenth century. In it, Parker, like other Western interpreters of the East to the West then and now, carefully lays out Hinduism's holy sites and suggests what they mean to the faithful. Twain often quoted directly from his sources, but he cherry-picked from Parker's book, linking the sites Parker describes to filth and disease. The upshot is a portrait of Hindu pilgrims, temples, shrines, and clerics that tracks the British contention that Hinduism was inherently irrational and that Hindus needed to be saved from themselves.

Today this section of *Following* comes across as intentionally mean-spirited, especially Twain's mock agenda for a religious pilgrimage. These chapters offend Hindus and frustrate Twain scholars like me who want to promote Twain's better side. This is another of the places where my relationship to Twain gets edgy—there are times when being a Mark Twain scholar is a lot like having an uncle with a penchant for politically incorrect jokes. You love him but avoid introducing him to your friends because you're afraid he will say something really insulting. That's the Mark Twain we see in Benares. I'd like to gloss over his more egregious cultural offenses, but they are glaringly present, so here goes.

Twain sets the tone for his assault in chapter 50, where he elicits his Western readers' sympathy by confessing that Hinduism is beyond him. "I should have been glad to acquire some sort of idea of Hindoo theology," he comments, "but the difficulties of it were too great, the matter was too intricate. Even the mere A, B, C of it is baffling" (*FE* 481). According to Dwayne Eutsey, Twain did later master some of the basics of Hindu theology and cosmology, primarily through hard reading in some of the "crossover" books being produced for Westerners by Hindu scholars such as Sri Ramakrishna, and through conversations with his friend Moncure Conway, himself deeply immersed in the study of Eastern religions. But all that came later, well after the publication of *Following the Equator*. Unable to give his study of the religion enough time for it to begin to make sense, during the writing of *Following* Twain eschewed theological exploration, turning instead to caricature. Knowing that Westerners already regarded the Hindu pantheon as chaotic, he imposed an order that would make sense to his readers. In other words, he converted his data into Western terms. And being Mark Twain, he did it through satire.

Twain's satire in these chapters engages the confrontation between Eastern and Western concepts of both spiritual and physical health. The assault accelerates in chapter 51, where Twain focuses on the Hindu faithful's indifference to health and sanitation. He knew his readers would pick up these cues because they were accustomed to hearing health and sanitation issues being hotly debated at home—back in the mid-nineteenth century Louis Pasteur and Robert Koch had discovered that bacteria cause disease, and the United States, with most of western Europe, spent the rest of the century (and a lot of the twentieth) coming to grips with germ theory and its ramifications for public health.[6] I'll be discussing the British narrative about India's resistance to public health measures more later; for now, let's just note that most of Twain's observations about Hinduism in Benares are filtered through it. He begins with pilgrimage, Benares's major business. Bringing his Western passion for order to the pilgrim circuit's seeming disorder, he lays out an "Itinerary" for pilgrims that leads from one site to another in a mock-logical progression. The Itinerary is meant from the start to be a joke, but it backfires, at least for anyone who cares what Hindus might think about being represented this way.

I've read most of Twain's works many times, and I have unpacked his language over and over. I'm still discovering what it does and how he does it. The more closely I read Twain's "Itinerary," the more I see how many functions—some of them counterproductive—its wording performs. First—and this is typical of him—Twain signals that what follows might not be unvarnished truth. "I got some of the facts from conversations with the Rev. Mr. Parker and the others from his Guide to Benares; they are therefore trustworthy," he claims (FE 484). I don't ever trust sentences like that—I think they come right out of Twain's authorial birth in American folktale traditions, where the storyteller's claim to "truth"— his "trust me" moment—signals that he's about to tell a whopping big lie. But Twain isn't casting doubt on his own veracity here; he's casting it on Parker's—which makes me wonder just how much he trusted Parker's qualifications for telling Benares's story. Twain's history of satirizing both guides and guidebooks suggests the likelihood that he didn't take Parker's word as final.

Which didn't stop him from appropriating Parker's text, including Parker's point of view. Twain's revision amplifies rather than critiques Parker's Western take on Hindu worship. As we saw in the Jain temple episode, the entire Clemens family was trying to understand how stone images functioned in the religions they were encountering. For American Protestants of the era, this was a genuine struggle. "The heathen in his blindness bows down to wood & stone" is a line from Reginald

Heber's well-known "Missionary" hymn, most commonly referred to by its first line, "From Greenland's Icy Mountains." (The hymn is also the source of the line "where every prospect pleases, and only man is vile.") It was a hymn so commonly sung in Protestant churches that the reference—think of it as a nineteenth-century meme—would have popped up in most visitors' minds as they toured temples and shrines.[7] I suspect it may be the single most significant obstacle to Western comprehension of Hindu worship (not to speak of one of the building blocks of US anti-Catholicism). Samuel Clemens certainly knew the hymn. References to it frequent his writings, and the "heathen in his blindness" line appears in the notebook Twain kept in India.[8] Twain's retrospective difficulty linking the "inadequate idol" in the Jain temple to the "subtle" intellectualism of Jain metaphysics suggests that the hymn blocked his ability to get beyond the images, both in his memory of the Jain temple and, later, in his assessment of Hinduism. Despite Mr. Gandhi's attempt to explain that for Jains, the images of the Tirthankaras were not gods, Twain failed to grasp the subtleties of representational worship. In *Darśan: Seeing the Divine Image in India*, Diana Eck notes that Hindus go to temple not to worship an image, but to "see"—*darśan*—the representation of the deity. In Hinduism the image is not the deity, but the deity is present in the image. It is important to go to the temple or shrine to see the image because one's gaze sees through the material object to the divinity imbuing it, a form of both touching and knowing. Seeing is insight: "Through the eyes," Eck tells us, "one gains the blessings of the divine" (3). Twain never got this kind of information, or he couldn't absorb it if he did; his comments on Benares consistently indicate that he still understood Hindus to be praying to objects rather than to powers that the objects represented.

Even more prominent in Twain's writing about Benares is the linking of water with filth and disease. This linkage, too, came from his British hosts: the British were working hard to bring germ theory to India, and Benares, with its (even then) highly polluted Ganges River, was a focal point of their attempts to establish public health initiatives. But because they refused to compromise with Hinduism's own understanding of "pollution"—as an internal, spiritual affliction that can be cleansed by immersion in Mother Ganga, among other methods—the British drive for sanitation incurred vociferous protest from Benares's Hindu community. The protest in turn fed into the government's long-standing fear of rebellion—the uprising of 1857, which the British called the Sepoy Rebellion, was still fresh in their minds, and the Indian National Congress, already a decade old in 1896, was calling for Independence. Determined to hold on to the subcontinent at all costs, the British waged a public relations war calculated to convince the world (and as many Indians as possible) that they were the most fit to guide India into the modern era. Hindu opposition to public health measures on religious grounds fueled the British argument that Indians simply didn't know what was best for them. Benares's polluted waters and frequent cholera outbreaks became part of the British narrative about Hindu irrationality.

Hence Mark Twain's "Itinerary." Most guidebooks move the reader from place to place by the sites' proper names: "The Acropolis" or "The Empire State Building," for instance—and follow the title with information about the site's history, architecture, or other pertinent data. In contrast, Twain titles his sites by their objectives—"Purification" or "Protections against Hunger," for example. Proper names appear, but with little fanfare; instead Twain focuses on the sites' putative functions, and he does so in terms that he knows will both repulse his readers and emphasize what he sees as the disparity between the sites' religious roles and their impact in real (i.e., Western) terms. Pilgrimage Site 4, titled "Fever," does this with admirable verbal economy: "At the Khedar Ghat," he records, "you will find a long flight of stone steps leading down to the river. Half way down is a tank filled with sewage. Drink as much of it as you want. It is for fever" (*FE* 485). Item 7, the "Well of Long Life," works both its adjectives and its ironies harder: the well, we are informed, "is within the precincts of the mouldering and venerable Briddhkal Temple, which is one of the oldest in Benares. You pass in by a stone image of the monkey god, Hanuman, and there, among the ruined courtyards, you will find a shallow pool of stagnant sewage. It smells like the best limburger cheese, and is filthy with the washings of rotting lepers, but that is nothing, bathe in it; . . . for this is the Fountain of Long Life" (*FE* 486–87).

You get the drift. And it gets worse: late in the chapter Twain notes that even Hindus who have performed all the correct rituals risk being reincarnated as an ass if they are so unlucky as to die on the opposite side of the river. "The Hindoo has a childish and unreasoning aversion to being turned into an ass," he opines. "It is hard to tell why. One could properly expect an ass to have an aversion to being turned into a Hindoo. One could understand that he could lose dignity by it; also self-respect, and nine-tenths of his intelligence. But the Hindoo changed into an ass wouldn't lose anything, unless you count his religion" (*FE* 493–94).

Twain's "Itinerary" for Benares is one of a set of satirical guidebooks he produced throughout his writing life: he cut his authorial teeth on making fun of guides and guidebooks in *Innocents Abroad* (1869), and he

never forgot how well it worked for him. So it is possible that in the beginning at least, he was writing to satirize Parker, but the section doesn't
come across that way. Instead it shows an American writer, immersed
in colonial narratives about subject peoples, pandering to an imagined
audience composed of Anglo-Americans only too willing to assume that
dark-skinned natives of far-off exotic lands are so gullible that they need
the firm hand of the Empire to protect them from themselves. We see
the same message in Twain's brief history of Warren Hastings's victory
over Cheit Singh in 1781. Singh was a local raja whom Twain records as
having refused to pay a fine levied on him by the East India Company,
which then controlled India. If Twain actually knew the details of this
story, he wasn't telling them; in fact Singh, who had already contributed
his contracted share of cavalry and cash to the East India Company's cof-
fers, refused Hastings's demand that he contribute even more, an act that
Hastings interpreted as rebellion. When Hastings tried to arrest Singh,
he fled. In retaliation, Hastings removed Cheit Singh from his position of
authority, leading to a series of events that culminated in the East India
Company's attaining sovereignty over the Benares region. All of this
came up during Hastings's impeachment trial in 1786. With Edmund
Burke leading the prosecution, Hastings's reputation as an administrator
in India was badly undermined. But—as is the case with political histories—by the late nineteenth century, historians had rehabilitated him,
revisioning the earlier generation's charge of corruption as a defense of
Britain's hold in India, and celebrating Hastings's seizure of Benares
for British interests. These are the historians Twain's own informants
read; as a result Twain defends Hastings, affirming that his squelching
of Cheit Singh's effort to refuse the Englishman's excessive demands had
"saved to England the Indian empire, and that was the best service that
was ever done to the Indians themselves, those wretched heirs of a hundred centuries of pitiless oppression and abuse" (FE 506).[9]

Today there are many guidebooks to help visitors appreciate Varanasi's history, cosmology, and spirituality, as well as thoughtful guides
like Manish. In doing my own postvisit research, I have been grateful
for the work of scholars like E. Alan Mirinis, Alex Michaels, James G.
Lochtefeld, Gavin Flood, and above all, Diana Eck. But in Cornell University's amazing Kroch Library—where three floors of a building that could
well serve as an airplane hangar are dedicated to Asian and South Asian
materials—I found two books that showed me what cultural work a good
guidebook can do. One is a real guidebook, and the other is a comic book
that trots us through Varanasi and explains what we are seeing through

its characters' questions. The comic book, *A Pilgrimage to Kashi: History, Mythology and Culture in the Strangest and Most Fascinating City in India*, is by "Gol" (Miguel Andrea Gómez), a Spanish historian and actor who also creates comic books. It follows the adventures of an Indian family who have come to Varanasi to bring a relative's ashes to Mother Ganga; the wonderfully illustrated pages follow the members of this secular family as they learn something about Varanasi's spiritual history and even more about themselves. One of Gol's collaborators is Rana B. P. Singh, and he, with his son Pravin S. Rana, is the author of the actual guidebook, *Banaras Region: A Spiritual and Cultural Guide*. Dr. Singh is a cultural geographer with a vita any academic would envy: professor of geography at the prestigious Banaras Hindu University, he speaks and publishes all over the world. His guidebook reflects his reading; deeply informed by "space/place" studies, he specializes in sacred spaces, studies of humans' relationships to divinity in specific geographical locations. His goal in the guidebook is to help readers discover Varanasi's genius loci, its spirit of place. "The process of understanding a place is a walk in search of interrelationships between the physical milieu and its metaphysical values" (18), he counsels, and the book positions itself as a "spiritual walk," a pilgrimage in itself, "a way and a companion on this march towards crossing and soul healing" (19).

Unlike the academic studies, most of which never find their way out of specialized libraries, these two "guides" to Varanasi try to bridge the gap between Western and Eastern sensibilities for ordinary readers and are readily available through online bookstores (I ordered both on my cell phone, through Amazon, that afternoon in the Kroch Library). Even though Gol is not Indian, he, like Singh, writes from an Indian perspective. I love comic books (discovering this one in the august library stacks made my day), and the lush imagery of *Pilgrimage*, coupled with a story line punctuated by histories and biographies, really works for me. So does *Banaras Region*. If I do make it back to Varanasi, I will take the guidebook with me; it frames its suggested walks and tours not only with their histories but also with a rich understanding of the significance of contemporary sights and sounds. I wonder what Mark Twain might have written if he had had these two books instead of the Reverend Parker.

Writing about Mark Twain is frustrating because he never stands still. He's an authorial shape-shifter: as soon as you think you know who he is, he turns into someone else. In *Following the Equator* one of the shifts happens right at the end of the Benares section, where he records an interview with Swami Bhaskaranand Saraswati, a holy man he believed to be a god. This was his second meeting with a putative god. The first had been the eighteen-year-old Aga Khan (a.k.a. Sir Sultan Muhammad Shah), who visited him in Bombay. The Aga Khan was a descendant of Muhammad and the spiritual leader of the Ismaili Muslims. Twain apparently believed he was a god, but he was misinformed. Islam is a monotheistic religion, and although descendants of Muhammad's daughter Fatimah and her husband, Ali, are honored, they are nonetheless considered ordinary mortals. Saraswati was not a god either; online reference sites refer to him as a saint, and Professor Singh describes him as "a great Hindu mystic and mendicant" who was "famous for his miracles and his service to suffering people" (111). Twain, however, described him as "a living, breathing, speaking personage whom several millions of human beings devoutly and sincerely and unquestioningly believe to be a God, and humbly and gratefully worship as a God" (FE 508). Although he cannot resist jabs at divinity's trappings—the swami's numerous names, for instance, and the prospect of a wandering deity's causing traffic jams—he reports his actual encounter with Saraswati respectfully and even a little reverently. The prospect of engaging in a life of simplicity, study, and meditation had to have some appeal to Mark Twain, a man for whom life's demands came so hard and fast that he could find peace only when he was cut off from the world on an ocean voyage. Moreover, unlike the stone images in the temples, the sight of a man who had given up the world to save his soul fit in with Christian narratives of renunciation, giving Twain a framework for understanding Saraswati's path.[10] Writing up the episode clearly shifted his own meditations into another mode. As I noted earlier, consistency was never Mark Twain's strong point, and we see inconsistency in full flourish at the end of this section. Notwithstanding his attack on Hinduism in the previous chapter, this one ends with a three-page commentary on respecting other cultures' traditions and beliefs, most famously in his declaration that "the reverence which is difficult, and which has personal merit in it, is the respect you pay, without compulsion, to the political or religious attitude of a man whose beliefs are not yours" (FE 514).

Sigh. Which Twain is the real Twain? The cultural attack dog, wielding cruel satire in the name of Western rationality, or the cultural ambassador, pleading for tolerance? I'm never sure, and that's both the fun and the frustration of working with Mark Twain. I can never predict where he's going to land. I do know that he moved in, and more importantly thought from, a privileged space that was white, male, Western, and Protestant. The intersection of those identities constitutes Mark Twain's constraint; whether hostile or sympathetic toward the "Others" about whom he so often wrote, he could not project himself outside that point of view. He wanted to—I think that's why he switches literary mode so frequently—but he was too firmly grounded in that base and too financially dependent on others just like him. I'm fascinated by the challenge his journey around the world presented to that worldview, especially India. How and why he responded expose both his own mental processes and the cultural narratives in which he lived. And though it's frustrating and a bit heart sickening to know that the author to whom I have devoted a good part of my professional life would have regarded me as (at best) an interesting alien, I know that it is precisely that clash of perspectives that frees me to see beyond Mark Twain's horizons.

2

Pollution

A Narrative

Hindu rituals were not the only phenomena that caught Twain's attention in Benares. He was equally interested in Mother Ganga, the river that epitomizes the difference between Hindu and Western notions of purity and pollution. The Clemens family enjoyed several boat trips down the Ganges, where they watched the pilgrims immerse themselves in the river. If guidebooks and stone imagery were the filters through which Twain read the pilgrims' itineraries, public health narratives were the filters through which he read their ritual immersions in Mother Ganga. "At one place where we halted . . . the foul gush from a sewer was making the water turbid and murky all around, and there was a random corpse slopping around in it that had floated down from up country," he records. "Ten steps below that place stood a crowd of men, women, and comely young maidens waist deep in the water—and they were scooping it up in their hands and drinking it. Faith can certainly do wonders, and this is an instance of it. Those people were not drinking that fearful stuff to assuage thirst, but in order to purify their souls and the interior of their bodies. According to their creed, the Ganges water makes everything pure that it touches—instantly and utterly pure. The sewer water was not an offence to them, the corpse did not revolt them; the sacred water had touched both, and both were now snow-pure, and could defile no one. The memory of that sight will always stay by me; but not by request."

In part because of Twain's report, and in part because guidebooks had warned us about Varanasi's filth, Billy and I headed there apprehensive about our health. We were told that human feces littered the streets, that the food would give us diarrhea, that malaria and other tropical diseases were epidemic. Remembering the cremation ghats on the Bagmati River in Kathmandu, where I spent my thirteenth summer, I was prepared to see charred corpses floating down the river. Meanwhile Billy, always conscious of his delicate stomach, steeled himself for a diet of plain boiled rice. None of our fears were realized. We had some of our best meals in Varanasi; the river appeared, if not clean, at least corpse-free, and the only shit we (I) stepped in was from a cow. To our surprise,

we loved Varanasi, finding the city and its people gentler and more courteous than those in any of the Indian cities we had visited so far.

Afterward we realized that we probably shouldn't have done so much
advance reading; websites in particular thrive on the sensational. Granted,
the city is old, it is crumbling, it is dirty—filthy even—and the area near
the ghats is full of touts. As in most Indian cities, the dearth of public
toilets means that humans relieve themselves outdoors, though not, like
the animals, on the streets—unless you count urinating men, a fixture
not unique to India. Even where toilets exist, much of the sewage flows
into the river. Crowds certainly spread disease, especially during festival
seasons, and the Ganges is not, *not* fit to drink, nor to bathe in. According
to Pryam Das and Kenneth Tamminga, Ganges pollution is composed of
sewage, industrial waste, the detritus consequent on bathing cattle in the
river, dead bodies, and surface runoff waste from landfills and dumpsites
(1647–68). Despite large-scale recognition that pollution is at a crisis level,
and despite years of top-down governmental planning to alleviate it, little has been achieved, in large part because the governmental agencies
haven't managed to engage the public in the process.

But engaging the public isn't easy, especially in places where there is
little consensus about causal logic and even less sense of civic responsibility. Solving the problem of Ganges pollution means bringing wildly different causal logics into some kind of communication, starting with the
concept of pollution itself. It's not that Varanasi residents reject science.
The question concerns *which* science, and how that science defines—and
remedies—pollution and disease. The city showcases competing medical
establishments: Banaras Hindu University offers tracks in both Western
and Ayurvedic medicine, and there are numerous astrologers, faith heal-
ers, and lay surgeons among the religious and general populations. But
each medical system is predicated on a different logic about the human
body.

For believers, Mother Ganga is the supreme doctor. She is the
answer to the pilgrims' quests; they come to her to be healed. Right here,
I realized, was the first obstacle to cleaning up the Ganges River: how
you define the word "pollution" depends on where you are coming from.
For Western-trained scientists, government officials, and the general lay
public, the word "pollution" connotes tangible, measurable, industrial or
animal waste *in the river*, a problem solvable through heroic measures to
remove the waste from the water and prevent its return. For believers,
however, the word connotes spiritual impurity *in the human being*, a problem solvable through meditation, prayer, and other spiritual and ritual

practices. One of these practices is direct contact with Mother Ganga. Pilgrims immerse themselves in the river because she has purifying powers; she cleanses not only those who bathe in her waters but also herself—including the sewage and other pollutants that invade her. In *On the Banks of the Ganges: When Wastewater Meets Sacred Water*, Kelley Alley notes that when she asked Varanasi residents what happens when polluted waters empty into the Ganges, they told her that the river dissolved the impurities (79). These contrasting ideologies of cause and effect show how difficult it is even to define the terms of the debate about Mother Ganga's future: if the believer knows that physical contact with the Ganges will purify her body and soul, but the nonbeliever knows that the believer's practices contribute to the river's pollution, it is almost impossible to find common ground on which to get the conversation going.

It's not surprising that Twain remarked on Ganges pollution in 1896. If he hadn't noticed it on his own, his British hosts would have pointed it out to him. Highlighting the conflict between science and faith was part of Britain's strategy to undermine Hindu legitimacy. The Hindus believed that the river was holy; British scientists did their best to prove that it was no different from any other. It was tough going. During his sojourn in Benares Twain even did a little digging himself: in *Following the Equator* he cites a scientific experiment suggesting that the river, highly polluted where raw sewage entered it, had purified itself a mile downstream—a study that slightly (ever so slightly) opened him to the suggestion that perhaps Hindus knew something that Western science did not. The experiment originated in the observation that cholera, common within Benares city limits, rarely spread to surrounding areas. Western scientists already knew that cholera was spread through contaminated water: in the 1880s Robert Koch, among others, had discovered that a comma-shaped bacterium was the cause of the disease, and by the early years of the next decade they had traced the process of contagion. The news quickly spread to popular science outlets. In 1893, for instance, British ophthalmologist-turned-medical-journalist Ernest Hart, editor of the *British Medical Journal*, contributed an article to *The Popular Science Monthly* that specifically traced the disease's path and laid its origins squarely at India's door. "India is the endemic home of cholera," he announced. "The heat, the moisture, the necessity of drinking stored water, and the habits of people that make that water foul, all combine to plant firmly in the district a *contagium vivum* of this disease, which enters man's body in the water which he drinks, and in return it enters the water by means of the sick man's discharges. A vicious cycle is thus set up" (634).

The scientists' challenge was to figure out why the disease didn't follow that path in Benares and surrounding areas. Since cholera is spread through contaminated feces, it should have occurred in communities downstream from the Benares conduits that spewed raw sewage into the river. The experiment that drew Twain's attention had been conducted according to Western science's standard methods. Dr. E. H. Hankin,[1] the scientist in charge, collected water from the mouths of sewers and from the vicinity of a floating corpse, measured the cholera bacteria count in the containers, and then dumped some of the bacteria into a container of pure well water. He measured the germ count in both containers again six hours later. Whereas the bacteria added to the well water had proliferated, those in the Ganges water had died. Repetition of the experiment consistently yielded the same results. After meeting with Dr. Hankin, Twain jotted down the following notes. Dr. Hankin, he writes,

> has proved that no cholera microbes [survive] in the Ganges & the Jumna. These waters kill them utterly in from 1 to 3 hours. Water below Benares & Agra contain no cholera germs; he got water from a floating corpse—he drove away a determined host of turtles & got it against the land where he could experiment.
>
> This is amazing. It seems to explain why the many floating dead do not carry cholera epidemics down the river. He says put cholera microbes in pure well water & they breed myriads in an hour or two.[2]

When he wrote up this episode for *Following the Equator*, Twain admitted that there was no rational explanation for Hankin's results. "For ages and ages the Hindoos have had absolute faith that the water of the Ganges was absolutely pure, could not be defiled by any contact whatsoever, and infallibly made pure and clean whatsoever thing touched it. . . . The Hindoos have been laughed at, these many generations, but the laughter will need to modify itself a little from now on. How did they find out the water's secret in those ancient ages? Had they germ-scientists then? We do not know. We only know that they had a civilization long before we emerged from savagery" (*FE* 500). Twain didn't try to explain this miracle; he cites it and then moves on. But as a writer—acutely aware of the tangle of knowledge and values compounding any version of any story—his comments betray his suspicion that Western science may not reveal the whole story. Even questions of pollution and public health wrap into the larger question of who is telling the story, to whom, from what perspective, and based on what premises. And the British narrative about Ganges pollution was definitely part of its propaganda battle against the East. I use the word "battle" deliberately; in talking about disease, the British consistently used martial metaphors, and they used them not only to discredit Eastern religion and culture but to stoke fears of invasion among Europeans. Reading the public health literature of the late nineteenth century in light of today's refugee and immigrant flows, which have prompted new nativist narratives about pollution and disease, makes the 1893 framework all the more glaring. Hart's "The Pilgrim Path of Cholera," for instance, manages to attack Hindus, Muslims, pilgrimage, religious festivals, and Eastern rulers together, all under the rubric of the necessity to "sanitize" the East in order to prevent cholera from reaching—and polluting—the West. The unspoken message is that the East stands ready to invade the West, to dilute its purity, pollute its cultural base. In Hart's writing, cholera becomes a metaphor for the threat of cultural warfare. "With cholera steadily creeping toward our shores, and all Europe standing armed against the invader," Hart begins, "it becomes a matter of the extremest interest, to inquire how the disease escapes from its home in India, under what influences it becomes able to break its bounds, invade the outer world, and carry death and devastation into countries where not only has it no natural home, but where it is so far an exotic that even after repeated attempts it fails to become acclimatized" (634). "All Europe . . . armed against the invader," "escape," "break its bounds," and "invade the outer world," carrying "death and devastation"—the call to paranoia could not be louder.

Having detailed cholera's transmission process in his opening paragraphs, Hart devotes the remainder of his seventeen-page article to stoking the fears to which his language appeals, building a panoramic survey of the danger to the West from what he projects as the East's filthy, ignorant, and autocratic ways. Like Twain, whose mock itinerary for Hindu pilgrimage highlighted the threat to public health posed by the polluted waters in which the pilgrims immersed themselves, Hart argues that religious pilgrimage and festivals launch the spread of cholera and other infectious diseases. Indians are innately "conservative," Hart reports. Their tendency to stay in one place generation after generation retards the spread of communicable diseases. Until, that is, they attend a festival or decide to go on pilgrimage. "At times of pilgrimage . . . all this isolation is cast aside, and pilgrims from widely scattered districts rub shoulders in the bathing places, wash and cleanse their bodies and their clothes in the same water, which in turn they drink in an unsavory fellowship" (641). It's not, in Hart's view, only Hindus who are culpable for moving around. Hindus come to Benares to cleanse their souls, at least keeping their germs within India; Muslims go all the way to Mecca, where "with a sudden crowding of sixty thousand people devoid of all sanitary knowledge into a country ill-equipped with sanitary appliances, governed by rulers whose chief principle and guide is a fatalistic trust in the will of Allah, the problem is complicated in a high degree." The upshot, according to Hart, is that "the fairs and pilgrimages of the East constitute the dangers of the West, and it is now recognized in every land that this danger is vastly aggravated by the greater rapidity of communication in these latter days" (642).

What is the Empire's role in preventing this spread? Hart suggests that England, in its imperial wisdom and benevolence, stood ready to save the day, no matter the difficulty. "Gradually England is undertaking the gigantic task of not only ruling India . . . but of reforming and remodeling her habits and her customs, a thing hitherto unknown, untried, and thought by many to be impossible. A solid mass of conservativism of habit and even of thought has to be moved, and has to be so moved as not to drift into anarchy and reaction" (645). And England, as usual, will go it alone, because its rivals, the Ottomans, are too cheap to fund their subjects' sanitary education. But even the shortsighted rulers are not entirely to blame. Their subjects are. "Nor would [the ruler's] people support him in such a crusade. To them Allah is great, and cholera is his will; nor perhaps does the evil seem to them so grievous as it does to us. To them who have to suffer Turkish rule a little cholera now and then may seem but a flea-bite." Talk about blaming the victim. Hart has mastered the genre.

"Turkish" here stands for what we know as the Ottoman Empire, still standing in 1893 and seen as a threat to western Europe and particularly to the British Empire, which, flanking the Ottomans, then controlled Egypt as well as India. The article is a brilliant example of the rhetorical distances to which the British went in order not only to thoroughly discredit the people, culture, and religions of its territories but also to foment fear and distrust of foreigners among its own people. It was a strategy that would prove effective over generations: as Priscilla Wald's *Contagious: Cultures, Carriers, and the Outbreak Narrative* (Duke University Press, 2008) suggests, throughout the twentieth century, "contagion" became a Western metaphor for spiritual and cultural pollution from the East.

Did Mark Twain buy into this narrative? By and large, I think the answer is yes. There's a good chance he had read Hart's article. The Clemens family had subscribed to *The Popular Science Monthly* since 1881. They must have valued its content, because in May 1891, as they were departing for a long sojourn in Europe, Twain made a notebook reminder about having their subscription forwarded to their new home (Gribben 2:554). So it's entirely likely that Hart's article reached them. And even if Twain didn't read Hart's particular article, there was a string of similar essays out there for his perusal. Military metaphors weren't the only rhetorical strategy employed to highlight the threat from the East; writers also marshaled arguments about "Science" versus "Faith," shifting a major site of conflict within the West into the global arena. Ganges pollution played into the narrative: when Benares citizens protested the colonial government's institution of Western-style public health rules, the administration broadcast their resistance as a case of fundamentalist Hindus rejecting science.

Within these contexts, it's hard to argue that Twain's chapters on Benares don't follow the Empire's party line. It was, after all, not very different from the public health narratives that had developed in the United States over his own lifetime. For the previous fifty years, as germ theory gained credence in the West, public health advocates and sanitary engineers like George Waring had striven to insulate cities against the spread of disease. The installation of sanitary sewage systems in large cities like London and Paris proved that human beings did not have to live in fear of recurring epidemics of cholera and dysentery. Mass media joined the sanitation battle, and plumbing, sewage lines, and safe water supplies all came under public scrutiny. Sam and Livy Clemens had embraced the campaign enthusiastically; their house in Hartford was equipped with up-to-date plumbing, toilets, and running water, and one reason they spent long summers in Livy's hometown of Elmira, New York, was that Hartford was prone to warm-weather malaria epidemics. They also kept themselves abreast of current scientific developments. Livy had been an enthusiastic consumer of science news since before their marriage, and in addition to *The Popular Science Monthly* the Clemenses' library contained books by John Tyndall, Thomas Huxley, Charles Darwin, and Andrew Dickson White, among others. Twain's marginal notes prove that he read them. Popular magazines backed up the scientific community: not only *The Popular Science Monthly*, which started publication in 1872 precisely to meet the public interest in scientific developments—but also older magazines like the *Atlantic Monthly, Galaxy Magazine, Appleton's,* and *Harper's,* all of which initiated science sections in the 1860s and 1870s and all of which published Twain at one time or another. Thus it's not surprising that Twain understood germ theory and supported public health campaigns in the United States, or that the East's palpable lack of enthusiasm for sanitation controls fed into his understanding of what made India "exotic." What is surprising is Twain's willingness to doubt Western scientific thinking on the basis of Hankin's empirical evidence. It is one of the places in *Following the Equator* where we see a crack in Twain's faith in the Empire's self-justifications.

Dr. Hankin's findings may have an explanation, by the way. As I searched for information about the current state of Ganges pollution, I found an article on the website Spargel and Fraise that uses Twain's observations as a springboard for discussing the existence of bacteriophages, organisms that target and consume specific bacteria. The history of scientific interest in bacteriophages is itself a study in cultural worldviews: Hankin was an early theorist, but the science wasn't developed until the twentieth century. By World War II phage therapy was advanced enough to play a signal role in healing wounded soldiers, but although the postwar Soviet Union continued to develop phage therapies for agricultural and animal diseases, Western interest in them waned, and until recently, few pharmaceutical companies invested in the process. Now there is renewed interest, for three reasons: bacteriophages are far cheaper than antibiotics, they carry fewer side effects than antibiotics because they target very specific organisms, and they can be used in situations where bacteria have become resistant to antibiotics. Phages can also be used to repair environmental damage. Experimental studies conducted both in the Red Sea and off the Florida coast have discovered phages that target viruses that destroy coral reefs. Perhaps similar discoveries can help remedy pollution in the Ganges. At the very least, understanding of bacteriophages proves that some elements of the river actually do cleanse themselves, and it also shows why Dr. Hankin could not find living cholera germs downriver. Mother Ganga, it turns out, bears within her bacteriophages that target cholera germs. Industrialization and irrigation are undermining their potency, but these organisms do exist. Their presence, and an understanding of how they work, give hope that more environmental remediation is possible. So too do experiments with river algae. Many types of algae live in the river, and some of them consume carbon dioxide and produce oxygen that can facilitate both plant and human uses. Others absorb chemical pollutants, thus removing them from the river. Like the bacteriophages, the algae are threatened by pollutants such as detergents, which affect the purifiers' life cycles.[3] Their existence, however, suggests that they may be one avenue toward revising the river's health. So these days scientists are also looking at pollution mitigation through microbiological manipulation.

Perhaps a combination of phage and algae therapies can be developed that will satisfy both Western and Hindu purity/pollution narratives.

Twain's focus on the repulsive and irrational in Benares still drives most tourist guides to the city, heightening visitors' apprehensions and framing the numerous tourist mishaps reported on the web. That wasn't his own experience, though, and it wasn't Billy's and mine, either— perhaps because none of us stayed down by the river. Instead, we took lodgings in the cantonment, an area where the British lived before Independence. Remarkably, it is still a kind of open-country suburb. Twain's party opted for a small villa surrounded by fields; we stayed in the Clarks Hotel, which has existed in one form or another since Twain's time and which sits on the cantonment's edge, with easy walking access to the surrounding country and past the kinds of villas Twain and his family occupied. Twain writes of the quiet and ease of living within a walled compound; Billy and I found the pleasure of our location to be its proximity to open country. Hence we left the hotel's walls, on foot, as often as possible, strolling down quiet, tree-shaded lanes and greeting the occasional pedestrians who scrutinized but did not molest us. We had just come from Delhi, where we had stayed at a family-run hotel, in itself a growing pleasure. Just beyond its door, though, was a pack of predatory taxi and rickshaw drivers, screaming for our attention if we so much as crossed the threshold. Walking anywhere had been an ordeal—one driver followed us up an alleyway, berating us for not taking his cab. In contrast, Varanasi's quiet country lanes gave us freedom of movement, a huge, even visceral, relief. This personal liberty was our Christmas present to ourselves; we dismissed our driver and guide and treated ourselves to a day of napping, reading, and strolling. That included visiting the small shopping mall next to the hotel, where Indian families were indulging in a day of eating, socializing, and movie going. One item missing from the Western narrative about India is the fact that Indians like to party, and the Christian Christmas is just another excuse—even in Varanasi. The mall and many of the streets sported Santa Clauses and other Christmas motifs, including that great American pollutant, canned Christmas carols. So much for my scheme to escape the American Christmas by visiting India in December.

The British story about Indian pollution persists, despite India's separation from Britain over seventy years ago, and the Western press still filters information about contemporary India through the British perspective. For me the more interesting angle is how much Indians themselves internalized the British narrative, and how much of it remains a part of the story that many Indians tell about themselves. Seventy-some years after Independence, India is still struggling to create a viable national identity, and part of its problem stems from the very strength of the narratives that the British imposed. In *The Indian Equator: Mark Twain's India Revisited* (2013), Ian (Lord) Strathcarron suggests that India was far better run under the British, and I suspect a lot of Indians agree with him, if not openly. But if there is nostalgia for the Raj, it is at least in part because of India's failure to create a single national narrative that could engage the imaginations and galvanize the energies of all Indians, transcending region, caste, and religion.

Not that there aren't Indian national narratives. There are lots of them. The problem is that they tend to undermine rather than strengthen a positive national identity. Pollution—particularly of India's waterways and city air—is certainly one of these narratives; it's become a national obsession. So too are stories about corruption, both government and corporate. When I started bringing the two concepts together I realized that "pollution" and "corruption" mean basically the same thing. Both imagine bodies: pollution imagines a tangible body—a human body or a body of water—while corruption imagines a metaphorical body, such as the body politic. Both concepts also assume *change*. And the changes are defined very similarly, including "to change from an original form," "to make dirty," "to damage," or to "impair integrity, virtue, or moral principle." In other words, both concepts assume that there was an original body that has been changed for the worse. These concepts contribute to India's national narrative, and they also lurk behind Western fears about the East, where the influx of peoples with vastly different customs is predicted to corrupt Western cultures that, nativists believe, have existed unchanged for centuries.

Within India, the concepts lead to self-critique rather than to xenophobia. Pollution and corruption are closely associated in India's public mind; pollution, Indians claim, results from the failure of corrupt governments to clean up the environment. Addressing this accusation, in October 2014 the new prime minister, Narendra Modi, initiated a "Swachh Bharat" or "Clean India" campaign, publicly wielding a broom and invoking the Mahatma Gandhi's drive for public cleanliness early in the twentieth century. Environmentally conscious activists, especially college students, took up the call, reaching out to the public with art installations, skits, and social media. Subsequent articles in Indian newspapers and blogs lamented the campaign's faltering progress and indicted both government and the general public. Many admiringly raised the example of Singapore, where littering is severely fined. Yogendra Saxena, chief sustainability officer for Tata Power, one of India's biggest industries, blamed both government and individuals for the deplorable condition of India's public spaces: after calling for fines equal to those meted out in Singapore, Saxena accused Indians of lacking a sense of individual social responsibility. "Change must come from within," he demanded, "be it at individual or corporate level."[4] Professor Vasant Natarajan, a physicist, also compared India with Singapore, advocating public shaming in addition to fines. Like a number of his compatriots, Natarajan suggested that official corruption influenced public misbehavior: Indians "break laws here because they see their political leaders breaking laws with impunity, being corrupt with no fear of retribution."[5] Other Indians simply lament the dearth of concern for the public sphere. Sonal Kalra tells the story of a friend whose "'cleanliness drive' is to ensure that the car she drives is clean. . . . It suffocates her to see her car dirty, so she tosses [soiled tissues and burger wrappers] out of the car, dustbin or no dustbin."[6] Indians also blame traditional caste divisions for their behavior: as Saurabh Daga noted on the *Quora* blog, "in Indian society cleaning is supposed to be the lowest denominator profession, something reserved for untouchables."[7]

Many of the articles about public littering refer to India as "the filthiest nation on earth," and Indians seem to have internalized the identity. They tend to raise the topic themselves, without prompting. As the articles also note, few seem to consider their own personal agency in the matter. In Jaipur I spent a couple of hours waiting in a fabric shop while the resident tailor made me a *salwar kameez*. When you wait around in an Indian shop, they bring you tea and chat with you. This shopkeeper wanted to air his views about the incompetence of India's government, and he used trash as his example. According to him, trash was the government's problem; it was government's duty to enforce antilitter laws. "What about individual responsibility?" I asked. I've watched Kansas parents teach their children to throw trash into containers—the reason most Kansas towns I've visited are refreshingly litter-free. I agreed with my host that the Jaipur government should arrange for trash collections, but I also suggested that local families had some responsibility there, too—that change could come from the bottom up and the inside out, as well as from the top down. He didn't hear me. As the afternoon wore on I realized that we were speaking from parallel universes. Like the scientific and spiritual interpretations of the word "pollution," our perceptions of the relation between self and nation depend on the narratives of cause and effect with which we grew up. The shopkeeper imagines power lying out there, in a "government"; at the same time he believes that the government is as morally polluted as the environment is physically. I want to believe that power lies in a dialogue between government and the collective will; the narratives I imbibed imagine a government that does its job without bribes and a population willing to sacrifice individual pleasure for the public good.

All of which simply brings me back to the power of narrative to shape perception despite evidence to the contrary. Even a brief survey of pollution in the United States shows the naiveté of my own narrative; Americans may not like to believe that their elected officials are corrupt, but the progressive degradation of our natural resources and the fight against effective environmental laws should tell us that payoffs are commonplace, in whatever semilegalized form. I am currently living in Brooklyn, New York, near the infamous Gowanus Canal, whose pollution level may well rival Mother Ganga's. Despite designation as an EPA Superfund site, cleanup has lagged, while construction on the canal's banks has proliferated—mostly of million-dollar, multistory, multifamily residences whose sewage overflows into the canal whenever there is a heavy rain. American logics aren't anything to brag about either. The increasing number of magnitude 3 or greater earthquakes in fracking-happy Oklahoma (3 in 2009; 623 in 2016) suggests that it wouldn't hurt us to examine the logics driving the oil industry. If Mark Twain were with us now, he would be writing scathingly satirical indictments of government incompetence (New York) and corporate greed (Oklahoma).

Though he accepted the British narrative about India while he was writing *Following the Equator*, by 1899, when he rejected US rationales for annexing the Philippines, Mark Twain had learned how to peer around the edges of such narratives and ask what was really going on. The more I write about the continuities between the world he knew and the one I've inherited, the more I've learned to do the same. Twain's account of conflicting narratives of purity and pollution in nineteenth-century India points to the challenge we now face globally. There's no question that natural disasters like hurricanes, floods, and earthquakes are increasing. The problem lies in how we understand them. Our century has learned its lessons well from the British colonial experience; causation narratives—and their careful dissemination through mass media portals—have become the major business of competing political parties within nations and of competing cultural blocs without. East and West remain in ideological conflict, and many of the stories the West tells about the East follow the same narrative arcs as the stories the British told about

India. As with all narratives, what matters is less the narrative itself than who tells it, to whom, and for what purpose. Mark Twain understood this. In Allahabad he was told that the Ganges would cease to be holy after the next twelve-year festival cycle. Assuming that all such tales emanated from the money-hungry Brahmin priesthood, he could not see how such a prediction might benefit them. "But I am not disturbed," he added. When the time comes, "the data will be arranged by those people who have charge of all such matters. 'Brer Fox he lay low,' as Uncle Remus says; and at the judicious time he [the Brahmin] will spring something on the Indian public which will show that he was not financially asleep when he took the Ganges out of the market" (*FE* 470). The observation about data manipulation is as good today as it was in 1897. What story, by whom, for what purpose? The details of the narratives may change but the arc, and its mission, remain dismally the same.

3

Money Matters

Or, Gifts for the Dead

Varanasi, December 2013. It is 5:00 A.M. and Billy and I are in a row-boat, gliding up the Ganges River. With us are our guide, Manish, and an unidentified oarsman. We are still in Varanasi. Twain's British hosts treated him to several boat trips on the Ganges, so I have booked one for us. Twain's description of the city's riverfront is among the most lyrical of his writings, and though the passage of more than a century between his trip and ours suggests that much would have changed, I hope to get at least a glimmer of the Benares that he saw.

To my surprise, the view of the Varanasi waterfront from the Ganges appears much the same now as it did in 1897. Here is Twain's description: "The Ganges front is the supreme show-place of Benares. Its tall bluffs are solidly caked from water to summit, along a stretch of three miles, with a splendid jumble of massive and picturesque masonry, a bewildering and beautiful confusion of stone platforms, temples, stair-flights, rich and stately palaces—nowhere a break, nowhere a glimpse of the bluff itself; all the long face of it is compactly walled from sight by this crammed perspective of platforms, soaring stairways, sculptured temples, majestic palaces, softening away into the distances" (*FE* 496).

Despite his satire of Hindu rituals and his critique of sanitary conditions, Twain's response to India was generally rhapsodic. He was swept away by the color, the crowds, the extraordinary difference between India and the civilizations he knew, and as this word painting reveals, his enthusiasm carried over into Varanasi's built environment. In contrast, the riverfront made me pensive. When I look back at my journal for this trip I realize that whereas Twain focused on the landscape's architecture, I was most struck by its ambience. We had asked Manish to schedule our river excursion for dawn, the quietest part of the busy river's day. For me, experiencing the transition from darkness to light rendered a sense of the city's spiritual history. My journal entry tracked our movements.

> We move out from the quay while the sky is dark. Above the land-ing powerful lamps beam down from the buildings, sectoring the town into rays of light and dark. The light reveals the intensity of the

built landscape, the multiple, overlapping tiers of quay, terrace, and edifice. Beyond the quays the steps, or ghats, rise toward the town, punctuated by small plazas. Buildings surround these open spaces, proliferating as the eye moves upward. Smaller structures on the lowest tier—shops and temples—are painted ochre or red. Larger structures dominate the next tier. To our left looms a large edifice, perhaps the residence of one of the many Hindu princes who established homes along the river to ensure they would have a place to die in the holy city. A bright lamp beams from one of the palace's cornices, illumining the red carved tower of a Hindu temple below. The scene is still but not deserted; early morning is prayer time in Varanasi, and many worshipers, alone or in groups, have come down to the river to ask Mother Ganga's blessing. Some sit in lotus position, meditating; others stand in the water, arms spread wide and hands open, facing upward, or scooping water over their heads. Manish tells us that one group rescues fish from the fishermen. Every morning they meet the boats, buy the fish, and toss them back into the water.

Later, after our boat had reversed course and headed for its landing near the cremation ghats, my thoughts increasingly focused on Varanasi's role as a place to die.

When we draw abreast of the ghats, only a few faded fires are smoldering. I am struck by the amount of wood piled up in the nearby boats, waiting to be fed to the cremation flames. Two details stand out to me: first the general trashiness of the area. There is no attempt to beautify death here. Wood lies in haphazard piles, and grey ash covers the steps and buildings. The second detail is the intense green of the supply boats. Like the ashes, the buildings in this area tend toward dull grey; the green boats are a visual magnet.

After we landed, we walked through the narrow streets leading from the cremation ghats back into the center of town.

We walk through an alleyway lined with decrepit houses. Some are guesthouses for the dying, run by the government. They front onto the cremation grounds. The old come here to spend their last days in the presence of death, in the hopes that, if their lives have been virtuous, the act of dying in Varanasi will release them from the cycle of rebirth and transport them to Nirvana. I buy a postcard of Lord Shiva

Figure 4. Cremation ghat, Varanasi, India, 2013; courtesy of the author.

to send as a get-well card to a friend who has just had open-heart sur-
gery. My friend is Jewish, not Hindu, but Manish tells me that Shiva
is the re-creator as well as the destroyer, so I hope the card will help
my friend heal.

The riverfront inspired Twain to meditate on religion too, but less
about spirituality than about religious sociology. Whereas for me the cremation ghats were a memento mori, for Twain they represented religious
power, an aspect of established religions against which he had been railing
for years. He'd been snarking about Brahmin priests throughout his visits
to Hindu religious sites; the cremation ghats gave him a chance to comment on their power to extort money from the faithful. He begins by linking the city's built environment to its role as one of Hinduism's holy places.
"All this masonry, all this architecture, represents piety. The palaces were
built by native princes whose homes, as a rule, are far from Benares, but
who go there from time to time to refresh their souls with the sight and
touch of the Ganges, the river of their idolatry. The stairways are records of
acts of piety; the crowd of costly little temples are tokens of money spent by
rich men for present credit and hope of future reward" (FE 496–97).

From money, Twain moves quickly to priests. As I noted earlier,
Twain's portrayal of Brahmin priests is similar to his portrayal of Catholic

priests; I think that in his mind one priesthood was much like another. According to him the Brahmin caste is crafty, grasping, and venal, and its priests are out to extract the last rupee from the innocent pilgrims who rely on them to help their dead relatives achieve nirvana. Twain saw this in purely mercenary terms. "A priest with a good stand on the shore of the Ganges is much better off than the sweeper of the best crossing in London," he remarks. "A good stand is worth a world of money. The holy proprietor of it sits under his grand spectacular umbrella and collects his commission, and grows fat and rich; and the stand passes from father to son, down and down and down through the ages, and remains a perma-nent and lucrative estate in the family" (*FE* 480).

We've already seen Twain confirming Western stereotypes about Hindus; there's no reason to belabor the issue in this chapter. Instead I want to think about death, and death rituals, in both India and the United States. Twain attacked the Brahmin priests because he saw them fleecing the pilgrims; his critique is about institutional structures and money, not about theology. Trying to understand what triggered his ire not only took me more deeply into Hindu culture; it also brought me back home. India isn't the only country open to questions about the role of money in the relationship between the living and the dead.

When I started researching contemporary Varanasi cremations I stumbled on a recent video, *The Last Rites of the Honourable Mr. Rai*, which seems to bear out Twain's assumptions. The film, recorded and distributed by the Rai family in 2007, shows an elderly man's cremation on the five-thousand-year-old Harish Chandra Ghat in Varanasi.[1] The funeral pyre is built on the sand by the river, and the eldest son, appropri-ately shaven and dressed in a simple white dhoti, squats with a Brahmin priest, who leads him through the ritual while younger sons and other men stand, arms crossed, looking on. Postures matter here: the crouch-ing son shifts uncomfortably. I have a hunch that he is more accustomed to sitting in front of a computer than squatting near the ground. In con-trast, the priest squats easily. In this setting, he has all the advantages, and he knows it. About halfway through the ceremony he starts his pitch, threading his demand into the ritual by telling the son to repeat after him: "Om, I of the Bharaduaj family, for the peace of the deceased, gift all these things to the Brahmin priest." And he proceeds to specify what "these things" should be: "gifts of food, gifts of money, gifts of all kinds." When one of the standing sons reprimands the priest, reminding him that "your services were negotiated in a lump sum; don't ask for more money," the priest ignores him, looking into the eyes of the eldest son and declaring, "Giving alms to a Brahmin will give peace to your father. It is an act of devotion to your father." Softening slightly, the standing son responds: "I'll consider it." But when the priest immediately pushes his advantage and asks, "What about feeding Brahmins?" the standing son snaps, "That's enough, priest! . . . Get on with it!" In the end, the priest seems to extract a cow and at least 501 rupees in addition to his original lump sum. And he is not the only skimmer in this game: the boys who light the pyre demand an extra 250 rupees to get the fire going properly. After a brief haggle, they settle on 150.

Twain would love this video; it confirms everything he believed about priestly venality. I suspect the only thing that would surprise him would be the kickback from the family. And I wonder whether he would make a comparison, as I certainly do, with American funeral directors, who also insinuate that lavish spending on funerals signals devotion to the deceased. Money is central to both cultures' rituals; the difference lies in how the money functions.

The Last Rites of the Honourable Mr. Rai shocks American viewers because in our eyes, the priest's demands and the ensuing haggling desecrate the religious ritual and dishonor the dead. A lot of Americans look down on haggling; part of our illusion of cultural stability comes from our assumption that a fixed price rules out negotiation. This belief persists even though we routinely haggle over car prices, not to mention at garage sales. We also assume that bargaining is in poor taste, especially when mixed with religion; that paying close attention to how much things cost somehow sullies religious rituals. This is especially true for funerals. When my mother died in 1968, her sisters arranged for the funeral at Baltimore's only (read "monopoly") Jewish funeral home. When Dad arrived—flying up from Latin America, where he was working—he was furious. After years of living in countries where haggling was routine, he lashed out at the family for having accepted the first price quoted instead of negotiating fairer terms. They were fools, he said, and spendthrifts, wasting his hard-earned money. I was twenty-three, and this was my first close death; I was furious at Dad for throwing a scene. Now I see it as part of a long-standing culture clash. My aunts had done what they felt was appropriate; the German/English side of my family valued respectability above all else. Dad's Litvak clan, coming from poorer and rougher roots, felt the opposite: for them value came from having negotiated the lowest price possible. It was inevitable that the explosion would come at the funeral. Money, and widely dis-parate ideas about how to get and spend it, had been at the heart of my parents' disputes throughout their marriage; grief just brought their family differences into the open.

Studying American immigrant history has put the family quarrel into perspective for me. My nuclear family epitomizes the conflict between the first-wave German Jewish immigrants (bourgeois, respectable, cosmopolitan) and the second-wave, eastern European Jewish immigrants (working class, insular, suspicious). In a nutshell: when the second wave started to arrive in the 1880s and 1890s, the first wave looked down on them as unwashed, ignorant, and embarrassing. The German Jews had worked hard to establish themselves as "American" and felt that the newcomers were blowing their cover. Staring back, the Litvaks perceived the Germans as arrogant, conformist, and cowardly. Dad's snarling over money at Mom's funeral confirmed my aunts' fixed contention that not only was he a boor, his behavior confirmed gentiles' accusation that all Jews cared about was money. His sisters-in-laws' contempt only increased Dad's ire.

There's another historical facet to the funeral fight, too, one that crosses religious boundaries: American funerals have become occasions for conspicuous consumption, in which families are expected to spend lavishly. One of my favorite Twain stories is "Buck Fanshawe's Funeral," from *Roughing It*; in it the deceased's friend Scotty Briggs boasts that the funeral he and "the boys" are planning "ain't going to be no slouch—solid silver doorplate on [Buck's] coffin, six plumes on the hearse, and a nigger [sic] on the box in a biled shirt and a plug hat—how's that for high?" (*Roughing It* 64).[2] Clearly by the 1860s American funerals had already gone over the top. Money is the key; expensive coffins and headstones confirm social standing, not just of the dead but of the family and friends backing the funeral. Jessica Mitford's 1963 *The American Way of Death* opened a lot of people's eyes to this phenomenon, but it didn't much change the funeral landscape. I honestly think most Americans would like to honor their dead in simple, decent fashion, with or without ritual. But the funeral industry has so manipulated laws and prices that it is almost impossible to do it cheaply. Sentiment, hand in hand with respectability, is key to the industry's success. American funeral directors grow fat from their clients' belief that it's disrespectful to haggle over funeral costs. Deftly negotiating the space between the family's status anxiety and their genuine grief, the directors propose ever more expensive funeral arrangements. Our fastidiousness about bargaining is a vulnerability they happily exploit.

In contrast, bargaining is a way of life in India. People haggle with merchants until they reach a price that benefits both. Bargaining over funeral costs is all part of the economic structure. But in India settling on the price is actually a minor issue, at least as far as funerals are concerned. As I read through the literature I began to see that the really big difference lies in how the money "matters"—whether it signifies a simple fee for services, or functions within some more metaphysical arena. Even in the United States, purchases "matter" differently depending on the context. This is especially true for transitional events such as birth, marriage, and death rituals, and in situations where objects are gifted from one party to another. "Gifting" is the key. According to anthropologist Jonathan Parry, author of *Death in Banares*, "the important point about haggling in Benares is that much of this bargaining takes place over *gifts*" (142). When I go back to the video, I realize that the priest is demanding gifts, not payment. This throws the conversation into a very different arena than simple bargaining over, say, the price of fish. Social scientists have been pondering the differences between gifts and other transactions at least since the French sociologist Marcel Mauss published *The Gift* in 1925. A student of Sanskrit and religion, Mauss pointed out that gifts are different from other types of exchange because they signal spiritual or emotional relationships between the giver and the recipient.

Twain didn't know about gift theory (though he certainly knew about the ritual complexities of gifts, since he gave and received many of them throughout his life, especially during this tour around the world). He couldn't see payments to priests as gifts, only as simple exploitation of vulnerable families. But thinking in terms of gifts helps me understand Varanasi funerals. Unlike Christian or Jewish clergymen, Brahmin priests are not simply accessories in the funeral process—the guys who know the ritual that dignifies death and comforts the living. Rather, the Brahmin priest *represents* the deceased. As such, his job is twofold. First, to obtain the most tribute possible for the dead on whose part he is negotiating. Whatever gifts he negotiates are *for* the deceased—food, cows, clothing, cash—even though, in "reality," the priest is the one to eat the food, milk the cow, wear the clothes, and use the cash to put minutes on his cell phone. Because he is acting for the deceased, the priest's job is to make sure that the survivors "gift" their departed relatives to the utmost limit. Which brings us to his second function. The priest is not only caring for the soul of the deceased when he haggles. "There is," anthropologist Parry suggests, "an important sense in which the spiritual goals of the pilgrims and mourners are positively promoted by the material acquisitiveness of the priest. It is by sweating gifts out of them that the priests purify the souls of those they serve" (147). The gifts, then, help the giver purify his own soul by performing the duties of the child for the parent; the child's generosity advances him on his own personal path toward nirvana. As Twain noted, all funeral functions in Varanasi are "owned" by specific castes and families—these are professions that are handed down through generations. Many of the priests are assigned to work with families from specific regions of the country, and they keep books recording those families' genealogies. They don't know the families personally, though—or what they can pay. The funeral is an active, ongoing negotiation between the families and the priests assigned to serve them. Repeated bouts of haggling help a priest determine both how much his customers can afford and how seriously they want to honor their dead and care for their own souls.

Payment for Varanasi funerals, then, is a matter of honor, honor seen primarily in spiritual terms. Payment for US funerals is about honor, too, but in the United States, as Scotty Briggs makes clear, "honor" is social, not spiritual. In spending to honor the dead, the spender garners social approval for himself. "In order to know a community, one must observe the style of its funerals and know what manner of men they bury with most ceremony," the narrator of "Buck Fanshawe's Funeral" opines (*Roughing It* 247). That story was written many years before Twain's visit to India—*Roughing It* is Twain's 1872 saga of his years in Nevada Territory and California. "Buck Fanshawe's Funeral" is a wonderfully funny story that is more about language than about funerals, but it captures the emerging American propensity to make death an occasion for conspicuous consumption. In many American funerals, religion is only window dressing. Funeral directors may piously suggest that there is something spiritual involved, but the man who spends lavishly on a parent's funeral knows perfectly well that he is buying himself social approval. Billy and I have been through this three more times since my mom died: his mom, my dad, his dad. We thought we'd become hardened to the pitch, but we were overconfident. The funeral director who talked us into a blue velvet lining for my father-in-law's casket not only calculated that filial guilt would overcome our cynicism; he could also see that my father-in-law's second wife wanted the pretty quilting to set off the blue suit she had chosen for his viewing. Billy paid, fuming.

When he reported on his visit to the cremation ghats in Benares, Mark Twain was telling his Anglo-American readers about a ritual that he understood through both Christian and capitalist narratives—two Western systems that, in his view, victimized their adherents. After our last parental ritual, Billy enthusiastically agrees. Reading Twain, watching the film, and still twitching over family pressures to up the ante during his father's funeral, he may outdo Twain in his hostility to both countries' formalities. My experience of my dad's death leaves me in a slightly different place. Dad—true to his thrifty (or was it controlling?) disposition—prepaid for his cremation. All I had to do was find his receipt and take it to the funeral home. There was no ceremony, and if there was haggling over the cremation price, Dad had done it himself, which I am sure pleased him enormously. Dad didn't like the clergy any more than Samuel Clemens did, and he expressly forbade any funeral or religious ritual. What he didn't consider was the impact of his decisions on his children. No ceremony meant no rite of passage to mark our shift from child to orphan, no way to satisfy our filial duty, other than to conscientiously close Dad's accounts and give away his meager possessions. As executor of the will, I had the duty of flying to California and clearing out his room—a simple enough task, as he had already pared down to the essentials when he moved into assisted living. The brother who lived nearby helped me, but with no funeral scheduled, we told the other brother not to bother to come. All this was blessedly easy from an administrative viewpoint, but it provided no emotional outlets. Dad had been a vibrant presence in all of our lives; it was difficult to pretend that he could disappear with no ceremony to mark his passing.

I note that when Livy, Twain's wife, died in Italy in 1904, he had her cremated there, shipped her ashes back to the States, and then transported her to her family's plot in Elmira's Woodlawn Cemetery, where the interment was conducted with all due religious and communal rites. Clearly, when death hit home, Twain did not refuse ritual comforts, nor did he spare expense. For all his cynicism, he fulfilled his culture's spousal duties. His own body was not cremated; when he died in his house in Redding, Connecticut, in 1910 his body was first taken to the Brick Presbyterian Church in New York City, where thousands attended the viewing. He was then transported to Elmira, to be interred next to Livy's ashes in the Langdon family plot.

"We must take the position that burial is stuck to merely in the interest of the undertaker (who has his family cremated to save expense)." So wrote Mark Twain in the margins of his copy of C. F. Gordon Cumming's *In the Himalayas and on the Indian Plains*, one of the books he consulted when he was writing the India section of *Following the Equator* (Gribben 1:268). Twain didn't like undertakers any more than he liked clerics, and this is not the only place where he lobs potshots at them. But undertakers

are not part of the Indian landscape, and it is clear that Twain was making associations from Indian funeral practices to American. He wanted
to argue for cremation, but social pressure muted his commentary. He
had Livy's body cremated because that was the only practical way to
transport it across the ocean in 1904, but he doesn't seem to have considered cremation for himself.

So where does this leave us? For Twain, it meant resorting to the
conventional. Livy's funeral was not cheap, nor was his own. Funerals
are communal rituals that assure the living that they have fulfilled their
obligations to the dead and to the community at large. Religion imbues
the rituals with meaning; communal participation assures the survivors
that they are not alone. In subsequent years, graves keep individuals'
memories alive. Twain has no direct living descendants, so no great-
grandchildren visit, but Twain's fans do—and they leave visible signs
that they still care. The last time I visited, on September 12, 2018, Twain's
gravestone was adorned by an artificial white rose, several rocks, a handful of pennies, and an (empty) sample-sized bottle of Southern Comfort.
But fans do not contribute to cemetery maintenance, a demand that lasts
for centuries. The Clemens family plot in Elmira's Woodlawn Cemetery
needs regular upkeep from the city and from Langdon family descendants. A day may come when there is no one left to care for the graves.

Figure 5. Mark Twain's grave, September 12, 2018, Woodlawn Cemetery, Elmira, New
York; courtesy of the author.

Funerals—and disposal of the dead—continue to be a vexed issue, from financial, familial, and even environmental perspectives. The more elaborate the rituals, the more expensive the funeral, and the older the cemetery, the more likely it is to fall into disrepair. For my father and those like him, both funerals and cemeteries are a disgraceful waste of cash—a position with which I agreed until I put his directives into action. My visit to Varanasi four years later brought back my sense of loss; there at the cremation ghats, I realized that Dad's children needed a ritual. Bringing together Twain's and my father's commentary on funerals helps me put both into perspective. Twain failed to understand Hindu religious obligations because he interpreted Brahmin priests' functions through his suspicion of Catholic officiants and through his distaste for American undertakers. Dad failed to understand the emotional functions of death rituals in his anxiety to save his family the burden of paying for his funeral. Together the two men raise questions that every culture struggles to answer: about family duties, about priestly intermediaries, and about the role of money in the relationship between mourners and their dead.

4
Will the Real Savages Please Stand Up?

M y Aussie friends all told me I'd love Hobart, Tasmania's capital. It was a lovely seaside town, they said, with beautiful views. A great vacation spot. A place to relax.

Not for me. I found Hobart rough, even a bit scary. Maybe because people seemed so proud of being descended from convicts, which to me meant celebrating the kind of people who enjoyed beating up on my kind of people. Maybe because everyone in my B&B was so very white, a social environment that always makes me fear that they will discover that I'm not *their* kind of white. Or maybe it was just because on my last day it rained, a lot, and I had to check out early and stupidly downloaded an update for my phone that totally screwed up my hundreds of carefully collected photographs, and then my flight out was delayed, and I missed my connecting flight to New Zealand, and, and . . .

Not the best visit. But in retrospect, I realize that my nervousness about convict celebration was just one facet of my edgy position in the project I had undertaken: I was a Mark Twain scholar whose ethnic, gender, and experiential differences from my subject not only would have relegated me to the realm of "Other" in Twain's eyes, they also sharpened my consciousness of my difference from the white Australians among whom Twain himself felt at ease. In Australia, and Tasmania particularly, I was keenly aware that my responses to convict history and the history of settler and Aborigine relations differed from those of many of the white Australians with whom I spoke. They also widened the gap between me and Twain; in trying to follow Twain's train of thought as he sorted through those histories, I was confronting some of his most racially problematic sides. So when I study Mark Twain's writings about Indigenous Tasmanians, all while myself learning about the descendants of the communities he assumed had gone extinct, I am aware that I am not only watching him tell stories that navigate his own conflicting responses to a new and alien culture, I am also navigating between his, my, and our shared cultures' fraught relationships with the First Peoples that European descendants have done their best to supplant around the globe.

Whether from personal racism, a willingness to appeal to his audience's own prejudices, or simply his use of the racially charged language of his era, Twain's writings reveal his sense of white superiority. As with everything else Twain, however, his racial attitudes are inconsistent. On the one hand, Twain's visceral response to cruelty and treachery drove him to call out the atrocities of white colonial history. On the other hand, he knew that it wasn't in his own interests to antagonize his audience, most of whom were either descendants of settlers themselves or employed by colonial interests. Moreover, he didn't come at his subject matter with an unprejudiced mind. As in India, in Australia he brought with him a bundle of racial stereotypes that shaped his apprehension of the Indigenous Australians whose history he decided to tell. Twain believed he wasn't a racist, but his public and private writings all demonstrate that he held a set of racial and ethnic preconceptions that color his writings about most of the nonwhite peoples he encountered.

Kerry Driscoll's excellent *Mark Twain among the Indians and Other Indigenous Peoples* (2018) meticulously details the deep history of Twain's racial attitudes toward Native Americans, Australian Aborigines, and New Zealand Māori. Like many readers of Twain's work, she concludes that he carried an animus against Native Americans for most of his life; *Mark Twain among the Indians* suggests that the prejudice also affected his understanding of other Indigenous peoples. When I began this project I was interested in Twain's handling of the stories he told about Tasmania's Indigenous population—people whom he described as "savages" but also celebrated as patriots "matchless" for their courage. I thought—and still believe—that examining Twain's conflicting views can help us understand not only where he is coming from but also the conversation about "savagery" and "civilization" that was ongoing in the West at that time. As my research proceeded, however, I also became interested in how the descendants of those people tell stories about themselves today. This chapter, then, is about telling stories: Twain's stories about the Tasmanian Aborigines; nineteenth-century Western stories about Indigenous peoples generally; contemporary Indigenous Tasmanians' stories about themselves; and my own story about bringing my personal history to my research into both the Empire's "final solution" to the existence of Indigenous peoples and the resurgence of those peoples today.

Twain's boat from Australia to New Zealand stopped briefly—too briefly—in Hobart. Tasmania is known for Port Arthur, an infamous, early nineteenth-century convict settlement that began as an experiment in penal reform. I took a day trip out to it while I was in Hobart and was struck by the contrast between its monuments to human cruelty and the pristine natural environment in which they stood: broken buildings, gray stoned and heartless, set off by intensely green foliage and a dazzlingly blue sea—all seen through air so pristine I wondered whether this was how the world appeared before the industrial revolution. Twain didn't make it to Port Arthur; one hundred kilometers from Hobart, the prison, no longer operating and not yet a tourist destination, was too far for nineteenth-century transportation to do as a day trip. He knew about the place, though; by the time he got to Hobart he had read Marcus Clarke's convict novel *For the Term of His Natural Life* (1874), which details Port Arthur's horrors.[1] So he came to Tasmania with convicts on his mind. He did visit some ancient ex-cons in an old-age home in Hobart, but most of the chapter he gives to Tasmania focuses on the extermination of Tasmanian Aborigines.

At first I was surprised by this move. Even though Twain couldn't actually visit Port Arthur, its history was well documented, and it would have been a natural theme for him to pursue—especially after having read Clarke's hair-raising novel. He'd written about convicts in Sydney, and though he harshly criticized their treatment of Aborigines, he didn't really question the settler narratives that were in the process of becoming the continent's official history. Australian history, not unlike US history until recently, was and still is highly imbalanced; settler history is basically treated as the country's origin story, while Aborigine history—the story of the continent's actual First Peoples—is either ignored or marginalized. Convicts, despite being regarded as a "stain" on the settler narrative, were nevertheless part of the nation's evolving sense of a collective self. But on second thought, I realized that Twain focused on Tasmania's First Peoples because theirs was the story of the people who had disappeared, whereas the settlers, including Port Arthur convicts who had been "rehabilitated" and lived among them, were the people who survived.

At the time Twain visited Down Under, settler history was evolving into Australia's national history, and Aborigine history was being transformed into a subset of Australia's natural history. As the story told it, the settlers were the people of the future, whereas the Aborigines were the people of the past—overrun by development, like the kangaroos and the platypuses. Ethnography, then a new science, was busily rationalizing their disappearance by categorizing them on the lowest level of human development and casting them as exotics from the continent's past. Even though Twain regarded settler dominance as part of the natural course of events, he knew enough about the writing of history to perceive the conflict between the two origin narratives as a conflict about Tasmania's national identity. Moreover, the way in which stories about Aborigines were being told raised questions about heroism and patriotism that were increasingly on Twain's mind. The Governor's Proclamation Board provided the catalyst. Produced in 1829 at the height of the so-called Black Wars, the Proclamation Board is a pictorial attempt to communicate British law to native Tasmanians.[2] Its drawings tell viewers that whites and Aborigines are equal under the law, and that whites who kill Aborigines, or Aborigines who kill whites, will be hung. At face value the Board

Figure 6. Governor's Proclamation Board, 1829; courtesy of the State Library of New South Wales.

appears to signal a sincere attempt by the colonial government to declare equal treatment under the law.

We know Twain saw the Board. In Hobart he visited an early iteration of the Tasmanian Museum, where a copy of the Board was displayed. He reproduces it in *Following the Equator*, and it is one of the very few illustrations in *More Tramps Abroad*, the English edition of the book. But he didn't buy the neutrality story. In the course of my own research I visited the New York Public Library's Berg Collection, which holds the manuscript of *Following the Equator*, including sections that did not make it into the published book. One of these sections shows us exactly how Twain understood the Tasmania saga. "The English government began wisely and humanely in Tasmania," he observes. "Its clear commands were, that the good-will of the natives should be conciliated; that the whites should live in amity and kindness with them; and that acts of violence against them, and interruptions of their occupations must be rigorously punished. That was the home Government—England."[3] Twain then recapitulates the story of the hostilities' origins, with copious quotations from his sources citing specific instances of settler outrages on native peoples across the world—including an account by Cotton Mather on the systematic killing of American Indians by the English settlers in New England. Twain concludes the section on a broad note: "The chapter is an indictment of the Human Race. Not of the English, not of the Spaniards, not of any particular group, tribe or division, but of the Race. Apparently Civilization is merely Suppressed Savagery."

Some of these comments appear in *More Tramps Abroad*. In *Mark Twain among the Indians and Other Indigenous People*, Kerry Driscoll suggests that the iconography of the Board, which includes a drawing of a black man hanged from a tree, must have triggered Twain's associations with the lynching epidemic occurring in the United States during this period, and that the concluding drawings, of black and white families intermingling, were so patently idealized as to signal the failure of the English government's goals (302–3). Even if Twain accepted the Proclamation Board's good intentions (and note that he specifies that it was a product of the "home government," not the settlers), he learned enough subsequent history to recognize its uselessness. He'd already heard about the settlers' genocidal practices on the Australian mainland, and he was in the process of learning about similar atrocities in Tasmania. Although all the histories available to him were written from the whites' point of view, some were more sympathetic toward the Indigenous Tasmanians than others. So instead of pursuing convict history in Tasmania, he educated himself about the Black Wars, the early nineteenth-century period during which the white settlers hunted and killed almost the entire Indigenous population of the island. In *Following the Equator* he presents the history through the saga of one white man, George Augustus Robinson. Not only were Robinson's accomplishments fairly well documented but they also illustrated the complexities of heroism, patriotism, and historical perspective that intrigued Twain. I'd never heard of Robinson before I landed in Hobart, so my learning curve matched Twain's. I ended up reading both Robinson's and his critics' accounts of his exploits and then trying to figure out how Twain evaluated them. The process wasn't easy, in part because I couldn't determine how much Twain actually knew.

Here's an outline of Robinson's intervention into the bloody conflict between settlers and Aborigines in early nineteenth-century Tasmania. The Black Wars raged throughout the 1820s, with much bloodshed and hatred on both sides. By the end of the decade most of the original Tasmanians had been wiped out. The survivors, probably not numbering more than three hundred total, had retreated to the bush, from which they continued to harry the settlers. None of the white forces sent out to get them had succeeded; the Tasmanians understood the terrain far better than the settlers. Enter George Augustus Robinson. Not a military man, Robinson was a recent arrival, working as a builder in Hobart. Robinson thought he knew how to bring in the last of the Tasmanians without further bloodshed, and he received permission to try. He roamed the island for four years, talking the natives into laying down their arms and bringing them in in small groups of twenty or so. They were then shipped to Great (later renamed Flinders) Island and "civilized" until they slowly died off.

The story of Robinson and the Tasmanians exemplifies the challenges historians face as they shape their narratives. Was Robinson a hero who put an end to the wars and saved the last of the Tasmanians? Or was he a villain who talked the Tasmanians into trusting him and then betrayed them? How does the story shift over time, and how do visitors evaluate the stories they read?[4] Here is Twain's account, written some sixty years after the event and taken, at times cribbed, from James Bonwick's 1870 *The Last of the Tasmanians; or, The Black War of Van Dieman's Land*—itself published long after the events it recounts. Bonwick, a teacher and writer, published numerous books on topics as varied as anthropology, Egyptian belief systems, and Australian history. He was a staunch defender of the Tasmanian Aborigines; in both *The*

Last of the Tasmanians and its sequel, *Daily Life and Origin of the Tas-manians* (also 1870), he refutes white accounts of Tasmanian atrocities and shows how systematically the whites sought to decimate and defame the people whose lands they were stealing. Bonwick's account of Robinson varies between grudging admiration and outright distaste, and I think Twain took his cues from him. But watching Twain navigate Bonwick's narrative shows how Twain's own values at times skew Bonwick's presentation. Twain alternates between quoting Bonwick outright and retelling the events Bonwick relates in his—Twain's—own words, words that at times suggest a very different perspective on the Tasmanians than Bonwick himself maintained. The result, as often found in *Following the Equator*, is a story that carries more than one point of view.

Twain gives us Robinson's positive side first. Robinson, he tells us, "set himself this incredible task: to go out into the wilderness, the jungle, and the mountain-retreats where the hunted and implacable savages were hidden, and appear among them unarmed, speak the language of love and of kindness to them, and persuade them to forsake their homes and the wild free life that was so dear to them, and go with him and surrender to the hated Whites and live under their watch and ward, and upon their charity the rest of their lives! On its face it was the dream of a madman" (*FE* 260). Even this seemingly celebratory paragraph contains more than one viewpoint: the language fuses the white community's estimation of Robinson's mission—"he set himself this incredible task"—and Twain's perception that the Aborigines themselves would scorn Robinson's ultimate goal, that they should "surrender to the hated Whites and live under their watch and ward." The ambivalence continues throughout Twain's rendering of the story. For instance, he tells us that despite official skepticism, Robinson managed to assemble a group of "former convicts" and "tamed" natives willing to accompany him unarmed. These terms suggest both latent brutality (the former convicts, now members of the settler society and as such in contest with the Aborigines for the land) and treason (the Aborigines who cooperated with the whites)—a search party not to be trusted, at least not by the outliers.

On foot, Twain continues, the party tracked down the scattered groups of Tasmanians, persuading them group by group to relinquish their arms and come under white protection. Twain dramatizes the story of their initial contact with the "Big River tribe"—apparently the most formidable of the lot: "The redoubtable chief stood in menacing attitude, with his eighteen-foot spear poised; his warriors stood massed at his back, armed for battle, their faces eloquent with their long-cherished loathing for white men. . . . Their women were back of them, laden with supplies of weapons, and keeping their 150 eager dogs quiet until the chief should give the signal to fall on." Discussion ensued—apparently the natives were amazed that the visitors carried no weapons. Then the women took over: "Robinson's tamed squaws ventured to cross the line and begin persuasions upon the wild squaws. Then the chief stepped back to confer with the old women—the real arbiters of savage war." Driscoll notes that Twain changed Bonwick's descriptions of the women as "female guides" and their "wilder sisters" to the pejorative American term "squaws"—a sign that he was reading American Indian/white history and stereotypes into Tasmanian history (305). To her observation I would add two more: that the designation of these warrior women as "squaws" demonstrates the limitations of Twain's sympathies for the native Tasmanians generally, and that the women's participation in warfare—indeed, their roles as the "arbiters" of warfare—meant that in Twain's view, females who fought (and worse, who made decisions for men) proved that they were what the nineteenth century termed "unsexed" females, unworthy of the status of "woman." Despite having just published a novel celebrating the French warrior woman Joan of Arc (*Personal Recollections of Joan of Arc, by the Sieur Louis de Conte*, 1896), Twain still clung to very Victorian paradigms for virtuous women. So the outlier Tasmanian women were "squaws" because they were nonwhite female indigenes who fought back against their oppressors and made life-and-death decisions for their communities.

In Twain's retelling of the story, the women advised surrender and the men laid down their spears. Hugs and celebrations ensued. And so, Twain reports, "in four years, without the spilling of a drop of blood, Robinson brought them all in, willing captives, and delivered them to the white governor, and ended the war which powder and bullets, and thousands of men to use them, had prosecuted without result since 1804" (*FE* 264).

So much for the action. Twain's skepticism about Robinson's project emerges more fully in the next section. Up to this point his recounting of Robinson's strategies for bringing in the outliers basically follows the settlers' story, in which the actions of one courageous man end a prolonged and bloody struggle—bringing peace, prosperity, and the absence of impediments (i.e., natives) to white control of the entire island. Twain wanted to know what happened to their adversaries, and Bonwick, always sympathetic to the Aborigines, supplied him with his material. However, as soon as he focuses on the aftermath of Robinson's success, Twain switches from the white man's story to the black man's. And to do that, he switches literary mode. His account of Robinson celebrates him as a "solitary hero"—a standard military trope in Western writing generally and one particularly dear to the hearts of American readers (think Natty Bumppo). But in taking on the Tasmanians' point of view, he is no longer dealing with an individual, but with a group—a group that had lost the war. To tell the Tasmanians' story, Twain (again like his nemesis, James Fenimore Cooper) employs Romantic nostalgia, a literary way of simultaneously celebrating and lamenting a defeated people.

The concepts of heroism and patriotism provided the pivots between modes. Twain maintains that neither was a white prerogative. To Robinson's solitary heroism he counters with the Tasmanians' courage, calling them "the splendid 300, the matchless 300" who were "unconquered, and manifestly unconquerable. They would not yield, they would listen to no terms, they would fight to the bitter end. Yet they had no poet to keep up their heart, and sing the marvel of their magnificent patriotism" (*FE* 260). Bonwick had eulogized the Tasmanians, too, noting that the island's British representative, Governor Arthur, "rightly termed them a noble race," to whom "even their enemies cannot deny . . . attributes of courage and military tact" (226). Bonwick also used the term "patriotism" in his memorialization of the Tasmanians' resistance to white rule, and he detailed the natives' sacrifices to maintain their independence. But by this point Bonwick's narrative has segued into distaste for Robinson; he sees the white man as an egotist who took all the credit for capturing the Tasmanians, ignoring "the action of his own dark companions who had brought the warlike tribe in peace to his hiding-place" (224). My own reading of Robinson's papers is a bit different here. It's true that Robinson's memoirs and letters minimalize his party's contributions—especially the Aborigines'—but even he acknowledged the Tasmanians' courage. "These people . . . cannot and ought not to be looked upon as captives," he told the colonial secretary (Plomley 572). The secretary ignored his advice, shipping the group offshore to a place where they could no longer obstruct white progress.

Twain, being Twain, picked up on Bonwick's criticism of the settlers, much as he would do later in the trip when talking about Māori resistance to white colonization in New Zealand. This doesn't mean that Twain didn't regard Aborigines as savages—he manifestly did. For Twain, a "savage" was anyone who didn't participate in the material and moral structures of white Western culture. It was a blanket term that ignored the vast differences between Indigenous cultures themselves (but that also, interestingly, included white people who transgressed their own culture's moral codes). However, Twain's celebration of Tasmanian Aborigine courage does mean he recognized that even so-called savages had rights to their own land, and that they were acting patriotically in resisting invasion. This is one of the places where I am conscious of the values I bring to this text—I want to celebrate Twain's own courage, his willingness to step outside his culture's (and more importantly, his buying public's) prejudices and affirm the right of native peoples to their own lands and cultures. But as Driscoll points out, Twain never got to this point when writing about American Indians, whose history with whites parallels Aboriginal history—an example of the inconsistencies that tend to damage Twain's image in contemporary eyes. He can champion natives in other countries, but (despite the quotation from Cotton Mather) he consistently demonizes American Indians in his own writings—Injun Joe, from *The Adventures of Tom Sawyer*, being probably the best-known example. A few years after his trip around the world he would defend the Filipinos' battle for self-rule against the Americans, but he would never associate the Filipinos' case with Native Americans' concurrent struggles with the US government—cases that were reported in the *Congressional Record* and in mainstream newspapers right next to the news from the Philippine-American War that he loudly denounced. Too close to home for him to see it, perhaps? After all, Twain too came from a settler society. He demonized American Indians because, as a member of a white Anglo-Saxon family who had journeyed ever westward in search of the good life, he had inherited his forebears' justifications for occupying native lands. Driscoll traces the origin of Twain's aversion to Native Americans to his great-grandmother, whose story of surviving a 1781 Indian attack in Kentucky was passed down to her descendants (20–25). There were a few times in his life when Twain seemed to recognize that white settlers and the US Army were far more culpable than the Amerindians they displaced, but not many. Peter Messent, whose 1993 article "Racial and Colonial Discourse in Mark Twain's *Following the Equator*" took its cue from Toni Morrison's recently published *Playing in the Dark: Whiteness and the Literary Imagination* (1992), suggested that American race relations stood behind Twain's writings about Aborigines, and Driscoll's book extends Messent's argument. Her thorough analysis of the construction of both *Following the Equator* and *More Tramps Abroad*, including all the manuscript sections omitted from the published books, suggests that Twain recognized the parallels between US and Australian treatment of native peoples but chose to suppress it for both editions of his travelogue. Her study of Twain's marginalia in his copy of Bonwick's

The Lost Tasmanian Race shows how Twain shifted from an engaged and angry reader of primary texts into the careful professionalism of a writer mindful of the audiences to whom he would be marketing his book (Driscoll 269–74). Clearly Twain's own settler background—plus his reading in nineteenth-century ethnography and his consciousness of his audience—drove his framing of both Aborigines and their conflicts with the people who displaced them.

We don't often think of Twain in terms of settlers—not, say, as we do Cooper, or William Gilmore Simms—but even a cursory glance at the Clemens family history shows that they were part of the second and third wave, occupying lands whose original inhabitants had been uprooted and packed off to the territories. As a descendant, he would have inherited settler narratives as well as family histories. Settler and occupation narratives construct binaries: they celebrate pioneer grit against native fury, settler systems of order and rationality against what they project as the chaos of Indigenous ways. They are central to identity formation among the occupying group: offered through tales, songs, and official "histories," they take root early in life and become elements of personal identity, the patterns of thinking and feeling that define who and what you are. As such, they are so difficult, so painful, to outgrow that most people never do it, for instance contemporary Israelis who grow up believing justifications for establishing settlements in Palestinian lands, or Han Chinese who justify occupation of Uighur territories.

I think that the trip around the world helped Mark Twain understand the function of occupation narratives, at least outside the United States. The problem lay in finding a way to communicate his discoveries, which is why I am pulling literary modes into the discussion. As I'm using it, "literary mode" could easily be termed "literary mood"—it describes ways of writing that emanate from, and seek to pull readers into, a particular way of interpreting events—sentimentally or cynically, for instance. I bring the topic in here because I think mode choice is a major issue for Mark Twain, especially when he is writing about highly controversial topics, and it gives us insight into Twain's mental, and perhaps emotional, shifts. But modes are not equally accessible across time, and those accessible to us at any given period often dictate our ability to communicate our ideas. Mode choice becomes even more complicated when the topic is political, and in writing about colonial racism, Twain was certainly entering the political realm. He needed a way to talk about it that his readers could understand. In the late nineteenth century, discussions of colonialism tended to be conducted in the language of the colonizer—even the many nationalist intellectuals who protested imperial rule used the high diction and legal reasoning of the imperial powers they resisted, believing that doing so demonstrated their capacity for self-rule. In the process they distanced themselves linguistically from their less-accomplished compatriots. Twain did not use that language, though he was entirely capable of doing so. He was a popular writer, appealing across class divides, and he had to reach for a language that would elicit his readers' sympathies. Sentimentality, a literary mode that later generations would accuse of promoting false emotions, was one technique he regularly employed.

I've dealt with sentimentality off and on over my career. In addition to studying Twain, I have also written about nineteenth-century American women writers, and I was part of the academic cohort that started opening that arena to scholarly study in the 1980s and 1990s. One of the first issues we had to tackle was the accusation, promulgated by two generations of male literary critics, that women's writings were inevitably inferior because they were sentimental. (Some, on the other hand, held that sentimentality was an inferior mode because it was employed so much by women. The goal was the same: get women's literature out of the canon, even if you have to jettison a major literary mode along with it.)

The problem was that a lot of nineteenth-century male writers used sentimentality, too. The male critics never quite resolved that little contradiction, but they did manage to get the women out of the curriculum for a couple of generations. When we decided to bring them back in, we had to tackle the sentimentality issue, which really meant looking at sentimentality's intentions—what writers hoped to accomplish when they used the mode. As my colleague Laura Mielke has noted in *Moving Encounters: Sympathy and the Indian Question in Antebellum Literature* (2008), antebellum writers like Cooper and William Apess described sentimental ("moving") encounters between American Indians and whites as a way of positing a common humanity—of transcending the bitter rivalry of these contenders for the land. Similarly, many women writers used sentimentality to force their readers to experience their characters' emotions, to create empathy. In literature aiming to expose social problems—like the Indian question, or slavery—sentimentality could be a powerful tool. In best-case scenarios, it could even move readers to action.

Mark Twain was a master of sentimentality. He could use it to create empathy, or he could use it satirically, to make fun of people, cultures, events, and even the mode itself. In using sentimentality to describe the fate of the Tasmanians, Twain was calling on his readers' capacity for empathy. In the process, he also educated them about the strategy the imperial powers evolved to permanently subdue their subjugated populations—what I am calling, in a deliberate reference to Hitler's Germany, their "final solution." The first step was to ship native populations to "reservations" far from the white metropolis or the rural areas white settlers coveted. The lands given to the transplanted indigenes were often very different from those to which they were accustomed, so that they could not use extant skills to get back on their feet. (An example would be sending warm, wet-country farmers to arid, high-country terrain.) On the reservations they would be subjected to soul- and culture-destroying unemployment, malnutrition, and lack of support. To these were added ample access to alcohol and, later, to drugs. As a final blow at community morale, children were forcibly taken from parents and incarcerated in boarding schools far from home, where they were trained to become part of the servant class and taught to disrespect their parents and ethnic group, creating a truly alienated population. Over the course of the twentieth century this model would be used in Australia, the United States, Canada, and South Africa, resulting in fractured, psychologically gutted native communities to which the ruling powers then pointed as evidence that they were constitutionally and culturally incapable of adjusting to the modern world. Twain lived through only the project's early phase, but he saw where it was heading. Sentimentality—a key tool for abolitionists before the Civil War—helped him prove the project's inhumanity to his readers.

Extant accounts aren't clear about how the Tasmanians responded to the proposal that they be shipped off to another island. Robinson quotes one contemporary newspaper account claiming that the natives were "delighted at the idea of proceeding to Great Island, where they will enjoy peace and plenty uninterrupted" (Plomley 573). Bonwick's account differs: he quotes from letters written by the captain of the ship transporting them to the island, who recorded that the Tasmanians were seasick and depressed, and that they "appeared to feel themselves forsaken and helpless, and abandoned themselves to despair" (230). Bonwick also visited the Hobart orphanage housing Aborigine children who had been taken from their parents, where, he reports, they "struck me as being sickly and depressed, and I wondered not at the terrible mortality that had thinned their numbers" (231).

These lines provided the stimulus for Twain's sentimentality. Thirty years earlier, in the last section of *Roughing It*, he had described the crumbling of native Hawaiian culture under white domination, and his description of the demise of native Tasmanians echoes that earlier profile. The message is that Western civilization, even when well intentioned, can be deadly. On Great Island, Twain writes, the exiles declined because they "were not used to clothes, and houses, and regular hours, and church, and school, and Sunday-school, and work, and the other misplaced persecutions of civilization and they pined for their lost home and their wild free life. Too late they repented that they had traded that heaven for this hell. They sat homesick on their alien crags, and day by day gazed out through their tears over the sea with unappeasable longing toward the hazy bulk which was the specter of what had been their paradise; one by one their hearts broke and they died" (FE 265).

I said above that sentimentality can be used in many ways. The variation in the passage just quoted is Romantic nostalgia, and in many writers' hands, this tale would lead to a "tsk-tsk-regrettable-but-inevitable" conclusion, the "evolutionary" reasoning being that cultures that cannot adapt to progress and modernity are fated to die. I think there's a bit of that here, but there's also a twist, one particularly interesting in view of the progressive passage of American miscegenation laws during Twain's lifetime. After recounting the story of the Tasmanians' surrender, Twain comments: "They were indeed wonderful people, the natives. They ought not to have been wasted. They should have been crossed with the Whites. It would have improved the Whites and done the Natives no harm." He ends his recounting of Tasmanian Aboriginal history by noting that remnants of Robinson's captives lived into the second half of the century, when, in 1876, "the last woman died, and the Spartans of Australasia were extinct" (FE 267).

A neat, if lamentable, ending to the tale, one that fits admirably with Romantic nostalgic elegies for "noble-savages-done-in-by-modernity" narratives. It is a conclusion to the Tasmanian story that you still hear today: many Australians, including white Tasmanians, believe that the remnants of Robinson's bands died in exile and that native Tasmanians no longer exist. The narrative gave Twain the exit he needed; he could urge his readers to sympathize with the Tasmanians because, being extinct, they no longer threatened anyone.

It's not true, though. Tasmanian Aborigines not only exist; their voices are increasingly heard. That last woman's name was Truganini, and her image has become an icon in the battle for Aboriginal rights throughout Australia. Truganini was one of the native Tasmanians who helped Robinson make contact with the outliers, and she lived to regret her complicity in her people's exile. I first encountered her in the

Tasmanian Museum, where her image drew me across the room. Her face is printed on a T-shirt, and the label next to the display case told me that the shirt had been produced for Australia Day, an annual event celebrating the first British settlement in Port Jackson (now part of Sydney), in 1788. The T-shirt is black, and Truganini's image glowers from its upper breast. Beneath her visage a logo is printed across green, red, and yellow bars that read, in alternating colors and fonts,

> Australia Day
> Invasion Day
> Invasion, Murder, Rape,
> Dispossession, Deaths in Custody,
> Attempted Genocide.
> Celebrate . . .
> You're Joking!

Figure 7. Truganini, 1866, portrait by C. A. Woolley; courtesy of the National Library of Australia.

The fury of the logo is what grabbed me. In fact I was astounded by the anger radiating from the Tasmanian Museum's entire Aborigine exhibit. I visited the museum because I was hoping to see some of the items that Twain saw. I got lucky; we both saw the Governor's Proclamation Board. But the label for the Board that I saw was written by local Aborigines, descendants of Truganini and her compatriots, who bitterly point out the hypocrisy of the neutrality narrative. "Although the Proclamation Boards showed our Ancestors and colonists to be equal, justice was one-sided," the label reports. "Aboriginal men were hanged or jailed for crimes against the colonists, but no white man was charged for crimes against our Ancestors." Twain may have shifted from celebration to lamentation in his retelling of the Tasmanians' story, but the Tasmanians themselves are just plain angry. This is their chance to tell their own story, and they are telling it from their point of view.

The exhibit capped my learning curve about Aborigine/settler relations. The Tasmanian Museum was my last stop on my first pass through Australia (later I would make another trip, this time with Billy). The previous three weeks had been an intense process of information gathering and integrating, of thinking across large swaths of data, of revisioning what modern history I thought I knew. But my experience was also intensely personal, a jolt of recognition that has if anything increased my understanding of cultural marginality, of contingent privilege, of uneasy racial alignment. The mixed-race status of many Indigenous Australian individuals was all part of my awakening. It started that first morning when I reluctantly took myself off to Sydney's Australian Museum, where the Aborigine exhibit focused on the twentieth century. I had expected the exotic; what I found was the familiar: photographs of dark-skinned, neatly dressed 1960s students, confronted by angry young white men as they tried to integrate a local swimming pool; the same students loading banners and placards onto a Freedom bus; protest encampments outside government headquarters in Canberra, the capital; copies of legislation, too little and very late, recognizing Australia's First Peoples as citizens with all the rights accorded their white compatriots. In other words, the same images of the 1950s and 1960s battle for civil rights that I was accustomed to at home. My own involvement with the US civil rights movement had begun in the late 1950s, when dear family friends— Cecilia and Leon Bass—introduced me to Fellowship House and Farm, an offshoot of the Philadelphia Friends' Young People's Interracial Fellowship of Philadelphia. Unlike most of Baltimore, these were venues where black, white, and brown people could mix, eat, debate, work, and socialize on an equal basis. In the late 1950s I was in my early teens, and I experienced Fellowship House as a welcome respite from the racial tensions of daily life. Later, Western High School, Baltimore's all-girl, fully integrated public high school, provided an equally safe space for young women to get to know each other across the color line. By 1963 I was an Antioch College freshman, busing in from Ohio for the 1963 March on Washington. Over the years my companions and I celebrated as legal barriers came down. Indeed, *Loving v. Virginia,* the Supreme Court case that overturned miscegenation laws across the country, came one year before Billy and I married. So I had some acquaintance with the movement on US grounds.

Until that afternoon in Sydney, however, I hadn't realized the movement's extent and influence on Indigenous peoples worldwide—an insight that would be reinforced later, when I toured South Africa's Apartheid Museum in Johannesburg. If Twain's trip around the world taught him how widespread were the strategies for solving the "problem" of Indigenous peoples, my trip in his wake taught me that the civil rights tactics that I experienced on US grounds had become the model for Indigenous protest across the countries born in the British Empire's wake. Even the anger I was hearing was familiar. It was the anger of people—black people, brown people, people "in between"—excluded, marginalized, despised for being who they were. It was the margins fighting to repossess the center, to tell their stories their own way. Twain came to Australia when only white people had the power to tell Indigenous stories; I came to Australia when Aborigines themselves were learning how to create their own narratives, in their own modes and expressing their own values.

Voice has a huge amount to do with this. And by "voice," I mean who gets to control the media through which those stories get told. My experience was primarily with museum exhibits, but that doesn't discount the many writers, musicians, filmmakers, politicians, teachers, actors, and other creative people who are challenging—and changing—Indigenous Australians' positions in the national power structure and, arguably more importantly, in the national imagination. The museums themselves have entered bravely into the process. Unlike most US ethnographic museums, those I visited in Sydney and Melbourne have yielded major control to the native communities they are representing, and these folks are happy to tell you exactly what they think. I was especially fascinated by the videos, by the frank way that people talked about themselves as Aborigines in a dominant white society. So by the time I got to Hobart

I was somewhat prepared for the Tasmanian Museum's Aborigine display, but not entirely. Maybe because Tasmania's native community is fighting the "extinction" narrative, this modest exhibit voices more outrage about the past than the glitzier exhibits in Melbourne and Sydney. It also voices determination about the future. Nearly all the labels are written in the first-person plural, and their message is *We are here, we are not extinct, this is who we are. Pay attention.* Their dual claims to ownership and survival resound throughout the exhibits. A section on dance quotes Aboriginal dancer Leah Brown: "Our dances stem from our history, our culture, and other elements which we grasp from elders. It keeps our people and culture strong but it also helps educate the wider community that we have survived despite adversity." Another label informs us that the curators are using Indigenous words where available, noting that language reconstruction is part of an effort run by an Aboriginal community organization. Throughout, the exhibits reiterate the native claim to the land: "waranta makara lumini: been here forever."

Although popular lore still maintains that Truganini was the "last of her race," in fact Tasmanians are very much alive. Twain's suggestion that the natives "should have been crossed with the whites" in fact described the actual state of affairs at the time of his visit—one that Bonwick noted but that Twain chose to ignore. (Could he have sanctioned interracial unions in 1896—the era of *Plessy v. Ferguson?* I don't think so. Not if he wanted to sell the book, which he did.) He probably also refrained because the story is basically about rape, not exactly fare for popular, family-friendly publications, then or now. But rape, agonizing as it was, was also the means through which Tasmanians survived. In the early nineteenth century the islands around Tasmania were home to a motley collection of sealers, men from all over the world who came to kill seals and sell their fur. They routinely abducted Tasmanian women, often forcing them into prolonged sexual and domestic servitude. Inevitably families evolved from these unions. Thus Tasmanians survived as mixed race, and over time, their descendants managed to create a new life for their communities, one compounded of both native and imported cultural traits. According to Kay Merry, who has researched the relationships between Aboriginal women and the men who enslaved them, the sealers didn't always have the upper hand. The women, often expert sealers and fisherfolk themselves, taught the men what they knew and in turn learned the men's culture. The result was the emergence of a new cultural entity, neither imported nor Indigenous, but a self-conscious compound of both.

The new community was not passive. The Tasmanian Museum exhibit features a time line of Indigenous Tasmanian history, which told me that during the time Twain was visiting Hobart mixed-race Tasmanians were already beginning to organize, including establishing associations, community newspapers, and health benefits. Throughout the twentieth century Indigenous Tasmanians joined mainland and Torres Strait Indigenous groups to fight the white government's attempts to deny them access to political, social, and cultural power. It took a long time. In 1997 the Tasmanian government became the first state to apologize to the Stolen Generations, the Aborigines who had been kidnapped from their parents and forced into government schools whose stated mission was to destroy Indigenous identity and culture. It wasn't until 2013 that the Tasmanian Museum opened an exhibit that told the story of the Black Wars from both sides. The activism continues: not only are museum exhibits monitored by Indigenous groups; multiple Aboriginal organizations seek to control access to, and information about, Indigenous Tasmania. Perhaps because Aboriginal power flowered right about the time the internet also took off, information is highly accessible and mostly well written and informative. In fact, overall, Australian Aborigine websites, both those run by the government and those run by community groups, are some of the most informative I have visited. Moreover, the convergence of community activism and technologies comes at a time when the Australian educational system has decided that it is finally time to include First Peoples history in Australian history curricula, a mandate, according to a curator with whom I spoke briefly at the Koorie Heritage Trust in Melbourne, that was passed only in 2012. Since few teachers know this history themselves, museum personnel are working with educators to create learning tools. The result is an explosion of Aboriginal culture and self-presentation.

I was so impressed by the exhibit at the Tasmanian Museum that I asked to talk with its curator, Tony Brown. Mr. Brown brought with him two young women, one a curator, the other a trainee. All three were mixed race, and they viewed the exhibit as a multifaceted mission to revive native culture, encourage pride in young Indigenous Tasmanians, and educate the wider public about the history of native/settler relations. They all seemed surprised when I told them I found the exhibit "angry," but Liz, one of the women, smiled and said she took that as a sign that it was effective. When I asked about the museum's goals, Tony Brown told me that the ethnography curators want visitors to leave with a sense that Tasmania boasts a thriving Indigenous community, to—in his words—"get past Truganini" and the assumption that native Tasmanians are extinct. In a major shift of narrative control, the museum has brought in an Aborigine Advisory Committee, which makes sure that the stories told are the ones the community wants told—a strategy that puts them in the center of political tussles, both within the Aborigine community and between it and the rest of the population.

One strategy the curators are pursuing is the creation of learning packets for schoolchildren. And if they are as good at producing the packets as they are in face-to-face sessions with children, they should be highly successful. While I was at the museum, a group of young schoolchildren came through. They were not over seven or eight years old, a restless age. But they seemed mesmerized by their guide, sitting in a circle around him and paying close attention to his words. Their teacher sat with them, also listening. This was in sharp contrast to the eleven-to-twelve-year-old school group I had observed in the new, stunningly designed Bunjilaka exhibit in the Melbourne Museum. There, the teachers (all white) brought the kids (also all white) into the exhibit area and set them loose, positioning themselves at the exits, presumably to prevent their charges from escaping. There was no teaching or organization to the visit; the kids were just tossed into the space. I don't know whether this was a particularly nasty bunch before they came to the museum, but there they were hooligans, banging on the interactive exhibits, making faces at the videos, and shrieking with disgust at the ethnographic displays. Other than guarding the exits, the teachers ignored them. I guess this was the teachers' way of fulfilling the curricular mandate. If my informant at the Koorie Heritage Trust was correct, the teachers probably knew nothing about Aboriginal history themselves.

All this came as a revelation to me. It wasn't that I didn't know that conquering nations routinely—often brutally—subdue the people they conquer. As Twain himself noted, "all the territorial possessions of all the political establishments in the earth—including America, of course—consist of pilferings from other people's wash. No tribe, howsoever insignificant, and no nation, howsoever mighty, occupies a foot of land that was not stolen" (FE 623). And it wasn't that I didn't have a basic grasp of the history of US Indian policy, which included reservations, Indian schools—the works. I'd taught Native American narratives and I knew some of the signal events. I'd also seen enough Australian films—like *Rabbit-Proof Fence*—to know that a similar process had happened Down Under. What I hadn't realized was the extent to which the system, including its rationales, had spread across Anglo-American territories through the twentieth century. Kerry Driscoll credits Twain's trip around the world with his emerging grasp of the effects of colonialism on Indigenous peoples—a realization that would come to fruition in his anti-imperialism four years later. I've come to the same conclusion—we don't see much of the change in *Following* itself, but we can see it as Twain absorbs his experiences in subsequent writings.

The history of Anglo-American treatment of Indigenous peoples is slowly becoming accessible to the general public, but many people still don't know much about its manifestations, even in their own countries. For instance, when Marj, a New York cousin, visited me while I was living in Lawrence, Kansas, I took her to the small museum at Haskell Indian Nations University, one of the two institutions of higher education in the town. The exhibit gives Haskell's history, starting with its birth as an "Indian Industrial Training School," a place where Native American children, forcibly taken from their parents, were taught trades like blacksmithing and dressmaking. Marj is a lawyer, knowledgeable about first amendment law, a supporter of civil rights, and an avid consumer of contemporary political news, but this was her first encounter with Native American history. She was stunned. "How could I have gone through all that education and not known about this?" she asked. The answer is, of course, because it wasn't offered her. In our generation, at least for children growing up on the East Coast, American Indians basically didn't exist.

The ease with which I could learn about Australia's Aboriginal history suggests how present Aboriginal voices have become in Australian society and how effectively they are making their case. This was definitely not the scenario Twain encountered in 1895. At first I found Twain's claim that he had never seen an Aborigine hard to believe, but the Aussies I questioned assured me that by 1895 most coastal Aborigine groups had been chased to the interior, leaving the major cities apparently populated by both white and nonwhite immigrant groups. Those mixed-race Aborigines who stayed let whites assume they were anything—Indian, Arab, Portuguese, whatever—as long as it wasn't Indigenous. During the time Twain was in Sydney, a mixed-race community lived on the site where the Opera House now stands, but Twain clearly did not know about it. Only in the last twenty years have Aborigines achieved any level of public voice, with varying levels of kickback from the white majority. In comparison to the United States, the Aboriginal renaissance in Australia looks more like the US struggle for African American rights than like the US struggle for Native American rights. As my cousin's bewilderment suggests, in the United States, Indians trail African Americans and Hispanics on almost every count, including access to public voice and national attention. In both countries, recent immigration struggles have complicated the "Indigenous" racial struggles.

It took me a long time and a lot of traveling to grasp that the "final solution"—reservations, kidnapped children, deculturation, and malicious neglect—had been used systematically across settler countries, and that the people who implemented the system were clearly in communication with each other. I think a nineteenth-century version of my insight came to Mark Twain, too. "Travel is fatal to prejudice" is one of his more famous bon mots. I'm not sure that's true—a lot of people seem to travel to confirm their prejudices—but for anyone willing to open themselves to new ideas, traveling can radically reconfigure their world. Mark Twain wrote about Tasmanian Aborigines at the nadir of their existence, and his research into their fate jump-started his realization that colonialism as it was being practiced was morally wrong. I first met Indigenous Australians in 2013, when at least a select group were beginning to achieve cultural and political power—including the power to write their own historical narrative. The future lies in their hands, if they can get their acts together internally and then network internationally.

For me Mark Twain's retelling of the story of Tasmania's Aborigines, together with other First Peoples' histories that I was observing, began a theme that has carried throughout my journeys in Twain's wake. In learning about Indigenous history, both Twain and I began to see the strategies that modern nations have developed to deal with the conflicts between First Peoples and settlers. Twain observed the genocide—both the slow and the fast—through which newcomers clear the ground of existing populations; I have come to understand the legacies of the settlers' "final solutions" in the one hundred–plus years that have passed since Twain's trip. Today we are seeing two kinds of movements: settler invasions like the Han Chinese in Tibet or Xinjiang, determined to supplant native cultures with their more "advanced" civilization; and refugee flows, uprooted peoples desperately making their way across borders in search of safety and economic security. In the first instance, the settlers employ variations of the "final solutions" like forced boarding schools and prisons to control those resisting their advance—indeed, as I was revising this chapter I read a *New York Times* article describing China's strategy of imprisoning and surveilling Uighur Muslims in order to force them to give up their faith and culture.[5] In the second instance, existing populations resist what they see as refugee "invasions" by segregating the newcomers in camps and creating narratives portraying them as dangerous and unassimilable. The history of my own people records two thousand years of similar strategies, one of the reasons all-white environments like Hobart make me nervous. We may live now in the twenty-first century, but for the people classified as "Other," it's prudent never to take security for granted.

The wider I cast my historical net, the more I understand Twain's own ambivalences. Yet I also find some common ground that I didn't think we had. When I first started reading *Following the Equator*, I assumed that Twain's declaration that "civilization is merely suppressed savagery" was a clever marketing ploy, a means of shifting blame from the particular to the general and thus not offending anyone who might be prone to buy his book. I wish I could hold on to that cynical assessment, but I'm coming around to Twain's point of view. Not only have I recognized the strategic patterns in Anglo-American "final solutions" to settler/native conflicts; I see the recent surge in violence toward refugees as a variation on the territorial wars of the past and on the narratives evolved to justify them. When Twain wrote about Tasmania he was sympathizing with the indigenes against the European invaders. Today the descendants of those invaders see themselves as the natives, defending themselves against the alien immigrant hordes. What goes around comes around. The more I understand contemporary events, the more I understand the importance of Tasmania's past, and why Mark Twain focused on the fate of its First Peoples rather than on those who displaced them. His belief that his racial group was materially and morally superior didn't prevent him from recognizing that it failed to live up to its own moral standards. The history he traces tells us as much about the global crises confronting us today as it does about the world Twain encountered at the turn into the twentieth century.

5

Dreaming

How easily our dream-life and our material life become so intermingled and so fused together that we can't quite tell which is which, anymore.
—Mark Twain, "The $30,000 Bequest" (*Mark Twain: Collected Tales* 2:608)

M ark Twain was extremely interested in dreams. So are Indigenous Australians. Twain was a dualist, and he regarded dreams as alternate states of consciousness, an "other" life that he lived while he was asleep. Aborigines are not dualists, and for them, dreams are conduits, passages into what outsiders have come to call the Dreaming, the ongoing time of the Ancestors that overlaps with waking time but is invisible within it. Because they are conduits, dreams play a major role in Aboriginal metaphysics. Dreams also played a major role in Mark Twain's life and writings. Twain's understanding of dreams and the Aboriginal understanding of dreams are very different, but what unites them is the intuition that alternate states of being exist, and that dreams are the way into them. Thus Twain's education—and mine, as I traipsed through the cultures he visited—encompassed more than history and religion. It also exposed us to the metaphysical systems that stand behind religions and shape cultural consciousness—the very thoughts we are able to construct, our methods for understanding what we see, our assessing of significance.

This chapter is pure speculation. I'm pondering the comfort Twain might have gained from Aboriginal Dreaming concepts if he could have been exposed to Indigenous metaphysics. He certainly tried to learn what he could about Australia's First Peoples. He did considerable background reading for the Australia section of *Following*, including ethnographic descriptions of Indigenous life. His friend Moncure Conway may have suggested some of his choices. Unlike Twain, Conway had actually met Aborigines. In *My Pilgrimage to the Wise Men of the East*, Conway's own 1906 memoir of an 1883–1884 journey to Australia, New Zealand, and India, Conway records meetings with Australian Aborigines whose situation—as the impoverished, "disappearing" First Peoples—greatly interested him. Although the Aboriginal group that he met in Western Australia performed the war dances that seem to have been the settlers'

sole interest in native performance, Conway surmised that the men and
women with whom he spoke had a far more complex cosmology than
their white spectators assumed. "One need only read through Brough
Smith's [sic] book on the Australian aborigines to recognize the remarkable character of their legends and folk-lore," he remarks (103).

Conway must have been a discerning reader; I would be hard put to
find the legends and folklore R. Brough Smyth records as "remarkable."
Smyth's 1878 *The Aborigines of Victoria: With Notes Relating to the Habits
of the Natives of Other Parts of Australia and Tasmania* is a good example
of the kind of ethnography being practiced in Australia in the nineteenth
century. In his description of Aboriginal life-cycle events, for instance,
Smyth is at pains to select the most "hideous" (his word, not mine) practices, such as infanticide and cannibalism, to exemplify Indigenous life.
The last chapter, "Myths," comes as close to considering Aboriginal
thought as anything in the book, but not very far. Most of the stories
Smyth records are about sorcery, witchcraft, and revenge, supporting the
distinctly "savage" profile of Aboriginal life he has built up in his previous pages. A few origin stories are scattered among the more spectacular
tales; perhaps those are the ones that caught Conway's attention.

In any case, the book appears in Twain's library, probably one of
those he perused during those London months when he was putting
Following the Equator together. With works by the Reverend J. G. Woods
(who popularized natural science); James Bonwick, whose *The Last of the
Tasmanians; or, The Black War of Van Dieman's Land* we've already seen
in Twain's chapter on Tasmanians; the Reverend Henry N. Woolaston (a
surgeon-turned-clergyman who recorded incidents of Aboriginal resistance to pain); and most extensively, Mrs. Campbell Praed, from whose
1885 *Sketches of Australian Life* (also known as *Australian Life, Black
and White*) Twain quotes extensively, Smyth's ethnography rounded out
Twain's education in Aboriginal life. None of these books treated Aboriginal religions in much detail or depth, which is too bad. I think that if
Twain could have had some serious conversations with Indigenous elders
about how they understood dreams, he might have reformulated his own
understanding of the relationship between dreaming and waking life. In
the process, he might have begun to see that much of his anxiety about
appearance, reality, and creativity could be mitigated by seeing dreams
as conduits into a world that overlapped with his waking life rather than
as an alternate world divorced from it. In other words, exposure to Indigenous concepts about dreams might have helped Twain realize that his
struggle to understand the relationship between his sleeping and waking

lives was complicated by his dualism, his habitual need to divide phenomena into "either/or."

Twain's dualism has been a major issue for scholars almost since
academics started taking him seriously. Twain's "problem," to be reduc-
tive, was that he was a born dualist, suspecting from childhood on that
he had more than one self (scholars have long found the moniker "Twain"
significant here). He did not live with this supposition lightly; we see his
struggle not only in his late, "nightmare" manuscripts but also in many
of his doubled characters, who live in radically different strata of the "real
worlds" that surround them.

I've lived with Twain's dualism for a long time. It fascinated me when
I was younger. Like Twain himself, I wanted to figure out a way to resolve
it. We had different reasons for wanting to resolve it, of course. Mine were
detached, careerist, and crass: I was a young literary scholar, working in
the wake of the New Criticism; I wanted to make a case for coherence in
Twain's writings so I could get published and get tenure. Duality wasn't
a personal issue for me; I was removed, "objective"—academic. Twain's
reasons were immediate, personal, and philosophical. Because he was
born into Western culture, which rests on dualist assumptions, Twain
grew up believing that waking and dreaming life were two different
states, and that only one could be "real." At first he just wanted to know
whether his waking or his dreaming life was the real one. Soon, though,
he came to doubt the very nature of reality, wondering if all apparent
realities were only figments of the imagination. And with this second
question came a third: If reality is a figment of the imagination, whose
imagination are we talking about? If, as he increasingly suspected, all
realities were dreams, who was the dreamer? Himself? God? And finally,
was the Dreamer the source of all the pain and evil in the world?

Years later I realized that not only was I not as detached as I thought
I was, I was as much a product of a dualist culture as Twain. Worse—we
both were simultaneously dualist and *anti*dualist. We both assumed that
"reality" should be one concrete existential state, that individuals should
be integral and consistent persons, and that (in my case) literary works
should cohere into a unified whole. Our expectations were the problem.

Now, after some thirty-plus years of following Twain around, I've not
only accepted his dualism, I've understood how it fit into dominant Western narratives about the relationship of self, world, and consciousness. I
see that Twain's attempt to understand alternate states of being drove his
most energetic writing, especially when he was writing about "twains"—
for example all of the boy doubles in his fiction, like the prince and the

pauper, and the white-boy-who-is-"really"-black and the black-boy-who-is-"really"-white in *Pudd'nhead Wilson*. I've realized that the "twains" and the dreams are closely related: "twains" explore life in alternate social spaces; dreams explore life in alternate mental states. One of Twain's few cheerful—or at least, bittersweet—dream writings is "My Platonic Sweetheart," a short sketch recording a serial dream that, Twain claims, he experienced over decades. In it Twain, always seventeen, meets up with a sweetheart, always fifteen, and they kiss and converse. Sometimes the sweetheart disappears, sometimes she dies, but the next time he dreams the dream she is resurrected, still young and lovely—and loving. Most of his other dreams are more fearful: one series features a man, happy and prosperous and surrounded by a loving family, who is mysteriously transported to a world in which everything is taken from him. Twain's late dream writings reflect his sense that even his waking life was falling apart, especially as he aged and as death took first one daughter, then his wife, then another child. Western religion—especially American Protestantism—clearly could not comfort him.

Scholars interested in Twain's speculations about dreams have linked him to Sigmund Freud. One reason for the association is that both men were in Vienna during the last years of the nineteenth century, and both were writing about dreams. Some of Twain's most significant dream writings were produced during the twenty months he spent in that city in 1898–1899—the same period the young doctor Sigmund Freud was working on the research that eventuated in *Interpretation of Dreams*. According to Carl Dolmetsch, it wasn't just coincidence that both Twain and Freud were interested in dreams. It was a sign of the Viennese times. In *"Our Famous Guest": Mark Twain in Vienna*, Dolmetsch notes that dreams were a hot topic among fin de siècle Viennese. Dolmetsch sees the general interest in dream states as an aspect of the nihilism—the sense that nothing is real and that life is ultimately meaningless—pervading Viennese society during the period. According to him, Austrian nihilism fit into the worldview that Twain was developing, and the writer imbibed it through both general conversations and his reading of late nineteenth-century scientists. The reading wasn't lightweight. One set of papers Twain plowed through was by Jean-Martin Charcot, a neurologist who experimented with hypnosis and mental telepathy. Another was written by Georg Christoph Lichtenberg, a mathematician who suggested that apparent time collapses might be as "real" as what we regard as ordinary life. A third was from the desk of Johann Friedrich Herbert, a philosopher-psychologist who wrote about the structure of human consciousness (Dolmetsch 282–83). Freud, who studied under Charcot, was reading the same materials; clearly he and Twain had common interests. Still, there is no definitive proof that they actually conversed. We do know that Freud attended at least one of Twain's lectures, on February 1, 1898, and that they both attended a Theodor Herzl play a month earlier (Dolmetsch 266, 270). Dolmetsch speculates that the two probably met at social events, perhaps several times, as they frequented the same circles (265). Twain definitely had an impact on Freud—an admirer, Freud used a number of Twain's short works as examples in his own writings. Freud's impact on Twain isn't established. Despite Dolmetsch's heroic spadework, we don't know whether Twain was conscious of Freud or of the theories Freud was struggling to develop.

But the West does not have a monopoly on dreams, and Vienna may not have been the sole resource for Twain's speculations. India was another source, especially Hinduism, Jainism, and Buddhism. As we've seen, Twain trashes Hinduism and related Indian religions more often than he engages them seriously, but I think at least one concept penetrated, becoming the source of one of his most enigmatic dream-manuscript fragments.

I've already described the Clemens family's visit to a Jain temple in Bombay, as reported not by Twain himself but by his guide, Jain scholar Sri Virchand Raghavji Gandhi. I've also noted that I think that Twain's conversation with Gandhi regarding nirvana was significant for the development of his inquiry into dreaming. When he wrote this section of *Following*, Twain was still wrestling with the concept of nirvana; he was having difficulty reconciling Gandhi's assurance that a state of "perfect rest" could also be a state of keen, perfect consciousness. For Twain, "perfect rest" meant the ability to blot out consciousness, to dissolve into the universe. Instead, he discovered, for Jains the concept of nirvana meant the removal of sensory experience; a state in which, in Gandhi's words, the "veil" that keeps us from direct contact with "knowledge" is removed. Rather than unconsciousness, the subject has perfect consciousness, a perfect understanding of what constitutes existence. According to Gandhi, that was "the Kingdom of Heaven."

When I detailed this conversation earlier I did so within the context of idols, the "stone images" that, I suggested, blocked Twain's ability to grasp essential concepts about Jain and Hindu beliefs and rituals. Here I want to address the latent effect of Twain's afternoon in the Jain temple. Twain scholar Dwayne Eutsey has explored Twain's reading in Hindu philosophy and cosmology, reading that occurred after *Following the*

Equator was published. Eutsey argues, rightly I think, that Twain's friendship with Moncure Conway, who served as his literary agent in London, may well have influenced Twain's readings in Hindu thought. Conway and Twain were contemporaries, both having been born in the 1830s, and both would also die in the first decade of the twentieth century. Both were world travelers; both, at times, Freethinkers; both writers, and both avid readers of contemporary history, ethnography, and religion. Eutsey points out that Conway's long-standing interest in Eastern religion was likely to have impacted Twain, whose personal library contained books that had also influenced Conway, including Max Muller's 1883 *India: What Can It Teach Us?* (Eutsey 69). Twain also owned a copy of a 1905 book titled *Advanced Course in Yogi Philosophy and Oriental Occultism.*[1] Both, Eutsey argues, stand behind the *Mysterious Stranger* manuscript. The point is that although Twain dissed Hinduism while he was writing *Following the Equator,* he came back, studied, and rethought the issue later, much as he had earlier come back, studied, and rethought the issue of race in America. As a consequence, Eastern concepts, transformed into Western imagery, permeate Twain's late writings.

Unfortunately, Twain's improved grasp of Eastern metaphysics doesn't seem to have mitigated his creative anxieties. In the chapter Twain seems to have intended as the ending to his late manuscript *No. 44, The Mysterious Stranger,* he turns "perfect consciousness," unimpeded by the sensory world, into psychic torture. The chapter is a manuscript fragment, dated 1904. Twain's handwriting across the top labels it "Conclusion of the Book." If by "the Book" Twain meant the unfinished manuscript of *No. 44, The Mysterious Stranger,* the "Conclusion" comes at the end of a novel in which a Candide-like narrator has been disabused of all his received notions about human decency, fair play, and the nature of reality. Not only has he had to grapple with a Dream-Self, a doppelgänger who intrudes into his waking life, but the conclusion to his learning process is the discovery that he is the dreamer who dreamed the world— and that thus he is the source of the horrors that have appalled him. The upside is that his dualism is resolved: the universe is one, bounded by neither heaven nor hell. The downside is that it's all his fault. "You are but a Thought," his visitor tells him, "the only existent Thought, and by your nature inextinguishable, indestructible. But I . . . have revealed you to yourself and set you free." Freedom, it turns out, consists in realizing that dreams are the *only* reality. The narrator's fate is to wander in "shoreless space," dreaming up worlds that invariably turn bad. "Dream other dreams, and better!" the stranger advises before he disappears.

I have always been struck by this chapter. To me it confirms Twain's solipsism, his conviction that he was the author of not only his own troubles but of the rest of the world's as well. I don't think this was hubris. After all, he was a writer of fiction, therefore a creator of worlds—if God could dream a world, why couldn't he? And he manifestly did. That's why most people associate him with the Mississippi Valley—or perhaps I should say they associate the Mississippi Valley with Mark Twain. *The Adventures of Tom Sawyer* and *Adventures of Huckleberry Finn* created both a geographical region and boyhood within it. And even those early novels feature fearsome forces and characters that haunt their protagonists' dreams.

The big problem with being a world creator is accounting for the presence of evil. It's one thing for most of us to denounce evil in the world—we may feel a responsibility for mitigating it or we may delight in participating in it, but we don't see ourselves as having created it from scratch. I think that in his darker moments, Twain believed he invented it. Which to him meant, on some level, that he himself was the primal evil.

There is an "either/or" element to Twain's struggles that comes from his dualism. I said before that he was a born dualist, but I also noted that both Twain and I imbibed our dualism from our culture. Both are true. Twain was born into a dualist culture; it was all around him, embedded in the worldview that we Westerners inherited from the ancient Manichaeans. Black/white, good/bad, god/devil, republic/tyranny—the Western way of looking at the world is relentlessly dualistic. Sometimes I think Americans got it the worst. There aren't many gray areas in our moral universe, which means we don't really have the framework for perceiving the "both/ands"—both good AND bad, black AND white, male AND female, democratic AND authoritarian. That's why we have so much trouble with mixed-race and cross-gender folks—we lump them into one category because we simply don't have the conceptual, sometimes even the linguistic, ability to understand the fusion.

What does this have to do with dreams? Only that we categorize dreams the way we categorize everything else. I am either awake or asleep; this is my waking life or my sleeping life, my waking self or my dreaming self, the experiences that "matter" or the ones that don't. Freudian psychology tries to find the connections between the two worlds, but Freud's process pathologizes both the dreamer and her dreams. Jung's "collective unconscious" tried to transcend the self/other divide, but it never gained the traction Freud's theories did, in large part, I think, because Freudian psychology fits nicely into preexisting Western dualism, and Jung's does not. So it's not surprising that Mark Twain, despite his heavy flirtation with Viennese psychology, may have looked to other cultures to help him understand his dreams. He found one way in India, but he transformed the idea of nirvana as "perfect consciousness" into a very Twainian notion of "perpetual-creation-of-evil machine."

And that's where a heavy dose of Indigenous Australian metaphysics might have helped. Because in Indigenous thought, dreams aren't confined to the dreamer; they are conduits from the individual to the community, past and present. A website for a gallery specializing in Aboriginal art defines the Dreaming in terms of Indigenous concepts of time, space, and creativity. "Once the ancestor spirits had created the world, they changed into trees, the stars, rocks, watering holes or other objects," the website tells us. "These are the sacred places of Aboriginal culture and have special properties. Because the ancestors did not disappear at the end of the Dreaming, but remained in these sacred sites, the Dreaming is never-ending, linking the past and the present, the people and the land."[2] Not only do the ancestors stick around, inhabiting inanimate objects, but individuals can make contact with the Dreaming through their own dreams or other states of altered consciousness. In Indigenous metaphysics, human dreams are corridors into timelessness, where the individual exists as one element in a complex web of relationships that itself constitutes reality.

In their introduction to *Mythology: Myths, Legends, and Fantasies*, Janet Parker and Julie Stanton observe that the Dreaming's complex of narratives and concepts provides meaning and unity to human life, answering fundamental questions common to all religious seekers. And a seeker is certainly what Samuel Clemens was. His good friend the Reverend Joseph Twichell, who argued religion with him for nigh on forty years, knew that. Twichell put up with Twain's religious skepticism because he loved him, and for a long time he hoped Clemens would come around. "Would that the grace might touch him with power and lead him into larger views of things spiritual than he has ever yet seen!" Twichell wrote his wife in 1878 (Messent 2009, 70). Clemens didn't come around; in fact he moved ever further away from conventional Western religions. So what could exploration into the Dreaming have yielded for him?

If Twain articulated a philosophical formulation for his interest in dreams, it occurs in the penultimate paragraph of "My Platonic Sweetheart," where his narrator cries out, "In our dreams—I know it! We do make the journeys we seem to make; we do see the things we seem to see; the people, the horses, the cats, the dogs, the birds, the whales, are real, not chimeras; they are living spirits, not shadows; and they are immortal and indestructible. They go whither they will; they visit all resorts, all points of interest, even the twinkling suns that wander in the wastes of space. That is where those strange mountains are which slide from under our feet while we walk, and where those vast caverns are whose bewildering avenues close behind us and in front when we are lost, and shut us in. We knew this because there are no such things here, and they must be there, because there is no other place" (*Mark Twain: Collected Tales* 2:294–95).

"Sweetheart" was written in 1897, the year after Twain's trip around the world and in the wake of his daughter Susy's death. The next year he wrote "Which Was the Dream?," one of the first of the nightmare manuscripts to rehash his bankruptcy. There the protagonist, impoverished and dishonored by a business associate, languishes in an alternative dreamworld for eighteen months of "real" time. Other manuscripts— none completed—followed. One series, collected in 1968 by William M. Gibson under the title *The Mysterious Stranger Manuscripts*, features dreams, doppelgängers, and otherworldly visitors who manipulate human lives for their own amusement. That's where the long, unfinished manuscript of *No. 44, The Mysterious Stranger* appears. Gibson did the editorial spadework that pointed to Twain's intention to attach the short chapter labeled "Conclusion of the Book" to the end of *No. 44*. When the narrator finally learns that life as he has known it is all a dream, the Stranger (who calls himself "#44") disappears, leaving the narrator alone with his perfect consciousness—and perfect guilt. That's a heck of a way to resolve dualism.

Indigenous Australians work it out differently. For starters, they aren't as anxious as Westerners about the relative "reality" of various states of being and time. They also don't experience the sense of separation that has plagued Westerners at least since the Enlightenment. According to anthropologist Ronald Berndt, the Dreaming coexists with secular time, and both times are equally "real." Not only do humans and mythical beings "share a common life force which is sacred," but an individual shares the spiritual essence of the "particular mythic being with which he is most closely identified. He may even be regarded as a living manifestation of that being" (Berndt 10). These relationships place individuals in a complex social network. "Aboriginal peoples have several 'totems' which can be personal, family, clan or nation," explains Cathy Craigie, former executive director of the First Nations Australia Writers Network. "These relationships give you responsibility for those relations, so in many ways you are never alone."[3]

My reading, my repeated visits to museums, and my conversations with curators, historians, and writers like Cathy introduced me to the complexities of Aboriginal spirituality. I don't mean to claim expertise here; far from it. I know that I don't understand far more than I do grasp, and that I'm filtering the little I know through a very romantic lens. And yet I can't help thinking that Aboriginal metaphysics could have enriched both Twain's previous exposure to non-Western religions and his fascination with mental telepathy—the latter an element of parapsychology that was receiving a good deal of attention within the turn-into-the-twentieth-century West. It's not that Twain hadn't read about other cultures in which dreams were integral to daily life. Francis Parkman's *The Jesuits in North America in the 17th Century*, which Twain owned, read, and annotated in the 1880s, has a description of dreaming in the Huron community that sounds a lot like the scenario for some of Twain's later nightmare writings. "An endless variety of incoherent fancies is connected with the Indian idea of a future life," Parkman's introduction opines. "They commonly owe their origin to dreams, often to the dreams of those in extreme sickness, who, on awaking, suppose that they visited the other world, and related to the wondering bystanders what they had seen" (lxxxii). Parkman's framing is significant, I think; he's describing Huron religion from the same Western, Christian viewpoint that later ethnographers would adopt. Taking his cue from the French Jesuit missionaries whose history he is detailing (and whose documents he is reading), this Protestant American historian describes Huron beliefs as the grotesque fantasies of a primitive and benighted people. Twain did not comment on Parkman's description of Huron religious beliefs, but his annotations in other sections of Parkman's text suggest that he was thinking beyond Parkman's own frameworks, and the record shows that he was quite capable of appropriating sentences like the one above for his own uses.

Even more pertinent than his readings in ethnography, Twain's interest in mental telepathy had already blazed a trail toward understanding dreams as a source of creative ideas. Twain wrote two short articles about mental telepathy (which he called telegraphy), both in the 1870s, but he did not publish them until 1891. Both articles explore incidents that most of us have experienced: thinking of a friend with whom we have not corresponded for years and then getting a letter from her the next day; receiving a letter in a similar scenario but with the letter containing proposals that we ourselves have just been thinking or writing about; having family members finish our sentences; thinking of an old friend only to have him appear. In "Mental Telegraphy," Twain cites a number of these incidents, concluding that they present evidence that "one human mind (still inhabiting the flesh) can communicate with another, over any sort of a distance, and without any *artificial* preparation of 'sympathetic conditions' to act as a transmitting agent" (*Mark Twain: Collected Tales* 2:38). Twain's specification that these are living humans who are not using intermediaries is intended to signal that he is not talking about spiritualism, the practice whereby "mediums" called up the spirits of the dead by acting as intermediaries between the apparent and the spirit worlds. In this he was speaking of his contemporaries' profound interest in various forms of what we now refer to as parapsychology. The Psychical Society, begun in England during this time, was an attempt to differentiate between valid and fake forms of extrasensory perception, and respected psychologists like William James (whose 1890 *Principles of Psychology* was also in Twain's library) included mesmerism and spiritualism in their studies of extrasensory phenomena. Twain was dubious about mediums and their claims, but he believed in the likelihood of telepathic experiences, even calling for "the invention of the phrenophone; that is to say, a method whereby the communicating of mind with mind may be brought under command and reduced to certainty and system" (*Mark Twain: Collected Tales* 2:42).

Twain's speculations in the parapsychology realm also extended to creativity. Citing multiple examples of simultaneous discoveries—as when Charles Darwin and Alfred Russel Wallace, who, living on opposite ends of the earth, came to the same conclusions about the evolutionary process—Twain probes the wellsprings of original thought. Refuting John Fiske's opinion that simultaneous discoveries come about because the investigators are working with questions "which many of the foremost minds in the world are thinking about," Twain instead proposes that "*one* man in each case did the telegraphing to the others"; in other words, that only one individual actually made the discovery, but his thought process communicated itself to others (*Mark Twain: Collected Tales* 2:43–44). And although he doubted mediums, Twain did believe that objects might have a role in thought transference: "Inanimate objects do not confine their activities to helping the clairvoyant, but do every now and then give the mental telegraphist a lift," he speculated (45). His investigations led to his conclusion that the mind does not originate ideas; it only organizes them. In an 1897 letter to Sir John Adams, Twain wrote that he now believed that the mind "originates nothing, creates nothing, gathers all its materials from the outside, and weaves them into combination automatically, and without anybody's help" (Adams 202). Twain had just read Adams's recently published *The Herbartian Psychology Applied to Education* and was probably referring to (and misinterpreting) Adams's explication of Lockean psychology. The notion stayed with Twain; in *What Is Man?* (1906), the central character insists that "none but the gods have ever had a thought which did not come from the outside. A man's brain is so constructed that it can originate nothing whatever" (*Mark Twain: Collected Tales* 2:735).

"My Platonic Sweetheart" shows Twain working toward an inclusive theory of the relationship of dreams to waking life. If we put his dream theorizing together with his speculations about mental telepathy, we see a man for whom it is plausible not only that human thought emanates from the outside, but that waking and dreaming life might not be separate events. At the end of "Mental Telegraphy," Twain recounts an incident from which he infers that he had been asleep when he assumed he had been awake. After he sees a man come up the walk, climb the steps and approach him, and then disappear, only to be found within the house a few minutes later, Twain decides that he must have fallen asleep for the time it took the man to reach the door, knock, and be admitted. "During at least sixty seconds that day I was asleep, or at least totally unconscious, without suspecting it," he concludes (*Mark Twain: Collected Tales* 2:48). "Now how are you to tell when you are awake? What are you to go by? People bite their fingers to find out. Why, you can do that in a dream."

On the one hand, this incident makes me wonder whether Twain blacked out for a few minutes. His daughter Jean was epileptic, as is one of my brothers; I mention this personal detail because living with my brother has taught me that people experiencing seizures often have little or no recall of the time that passes while they are in their alternate state. So I wonder whether Twain experienced some kind of mild seizure himself, without knowing it. On the other hand, Twain's meditations on telepathy and dreaming also bring me back to thinking about Aboriginal metaphysics. Not only would Aboriginal understanding of the relationship of dreams to waking life have answered some of Twain's questions about which state of being was "real," but Indigenous understanding of the relationship between living humans and the Ancestors whose forces created the earth would have helped Twain think through his questions—and anxieties—about his own creativity. His meditations about the role of objects in thought transference are relevant to the Aboriginal belief that the Ancestors still inhabit natural objects, exerting influence throughout the centuries. His sense that thoughts come from without, that original thought is impossible, would have put his position as a creator, what the ancient Greeks called a *poetes*, or maker, into a very different category than we see at the end of *No. 44, The Mysterious Stranger.* Instead of being a unique individual, hanging out there alone in Western time and space, he would know that he shared the essence of one or more of the original creators, the Ancestors of the Dreaming. So the tales he told and redacted, the fictional worlds he invented, would not be his responsibility alone. With this, if he could imagine himself as a living manifestation of a particular mythic being (in Hindu cosmologies, I could see him identifying with Shiva, the god who creates and destroys), he might feel, rather than guilt, a sense of divine mission, his job being to create and destroy worlds until he got it right. And finally, he would know that he was not alone, and that death was not a disruption of life but rather another manifestation of being in sacred time.

Outsiders' grasp of Aboriginal religions has come slowly, in part because of ethnographers' resistance to taking Indigenous thought on its own terms and in part because Aborigines believe that sacred knowledge should not be shared with strangers or uninitiated members of their own clans. In the early through mid-twentieth century, ethnologists' primary interest in Indigenous culture was as a living relic of what they saw as *Naturvolk*, primal human groups whose lives had changed little over the millennia. In the early 1970s Mircea Eliade took issue with this view, faulting twentieth-century anthropologists for continuing to present Aboriginal culture as primitive and resistant to change. In *Australian Religions: An Introduction* (1973), he insisted that

> the fact that the Aborigines reacted creatively with regard to external cultural influences, accepting and assimilating certain elements, rejecting or ignoring others, shows that they behaved like *historical* beings, and not as a *Naturvolk*. . . . In fact, the distinctive characteristic of Australians and other primitive people is not their lack of history but their specific interpretation of human historicity. They too live in history and are shaped by historical events; but they do not have a historical awareness comparable, say, to that of Westerners. . . . The aborigines do not record historical events in an irreversible chronological order. The changes and innovations, which imperceptibly but continuously transformed their existence, were telescoped into the mythical era; that is they became part of the tribal sacred history. . . . Their sacred history is meaningful, not because it narrates the events in a chronological order, but because it reveals the

beginnings of the world, the appearance of the Ancestors, and their dramatic and exemplary deeds. (190)

Extending Eliade's observations into her own critique of Western metaphysics, in *Ancestral Power: The Dreaming, Consciousness, and Aboriginal Australians* (2002), Lynne Hume notes that in the West, "since the Enlightenment, the notion of other worlds and alternative realities has been progressively devalued by the importance of rationalism. . . . [The Enlightenment] emphasized the material dimension of the physical universe, to the detriment of the spiritual dimension" (5). Certainly this was the perspective through which Twain, for all his admiration of their arts and technologies, evaluated Australian Aborigines. It was the simplicity, which he could understand only as the poverty, of their lifestyles that did them in. With his contemporaries, he couldn't conceive of a human group voluntarily eschewing the material trappings of "civilization." The fact that Aborigines lived off the land, building only rudimentary structures and clothing themselves only enough to keep warm, baffled him. "They were lazy—always lazy," he concluded. "Perhaps that was their trouble. It is a killing defect. Surely they could have invented and built a competent house, but they didn't. And they could have invented and developed the agricultural arts, but they didn't. They went naked and houseless, and lived on fish and grubs and worms and wild fruits, and were just plain savages, for all their smartness" (*FE* 207).

Twain's evaluation is telling, given the ethnographic framework of his era. Smyth wasn't the only ethnographer to fault Aborigines for the simplicity of their lifestyles. Twain's definition of savagery here also reflects the writings of early anthropologists such as Lewis Henry Morgan, whose 1877 *Ancient Society: Or, Researches in the Lines of Human Progress from Savagery, through Barbarism to Civilization* divided, subdivided, and ranked human groups into levels of savagery, barbarism, and civilization. For Morgan, Australian Aborigines were "in [a state of] savagery, pure and simple, with the arts and institutions belonging to that condition" (16). In contrast to the Aborigines, "civilized" peoples constructed houses, "improved" the land through agriculture, clothed their bodies, and developed some recognizable form of culinary art.

And yet Twain also recognized the racism inherent in the anthropologists' rankings, sensing that there was more of value in Indigenous life than they were willing to admit. "It must have been race-aversion that put upon them [i.e., Aborigines] a good deal of the low-rate intellectual reputation which they bear and have borne this long time in the world's estimate of them," he observed (*FE* 207). He could see that Indigenous art deserved to be taken seriously, suggesting that it should not be "classified with savage art at all, but on a plane two degrees above it and one degree above the lowest plane of civilized art" (*FE* 218). Perhaps his reading of James Bonwick's works helped him appreciate the quality of Aboriginal art—one of the few white men to defend Aboriginal intelligence and morality, Bonwick appreciates Aboriginal drawings even when he does not know what to make of them. In *Daily Life and Origin of the Tasmanians* (1870), Bonwick notes the sets of curious drawings found in northwestern Australia, describing them as "human figures in long dresses" who had "a sort of halo round the head" and no mouths (48). Now known as the Wandjina figures, in fact they are references to the Ancestors, the beings who created humankind and who then descended into the waters' depths, where they continue to produce "child-seeds," the sources of human beings. In other words, the drawings refer to Aboriginal origin stories, to the beginnings of human time, and to the continued presence of primal creative forces in human life.

Which brings us back to religion, and to Twain's problem with alternative realities. These days, anthropologists are exploring the Dreaming from the viewpoint of human consciousness. Scholars such as Lynne Hume approach Aboriginal religion through a disciplinary fusion of brain science, explorations into altered states of consciousness, and studies of Aboriginal life. Hume begins by noting the differences between Western and non-Western concepts of "reality." Unlike in the West, where only one fundamental reality is assumed,

> in most non-Western societies people operate within the context of a cosmos composed of multiple realities. . . . [In these non-Western societies] all experience is meaningful, regardless of the phase of consciousness (waking, dreaming, trance) during which it arises. In fact, reality, conceived as existing at multiple levels, may be verified by being experienced in different phases of consciousness. Many Westerners . . . [view] the "normal" waking phase as the only phase appropriate to the accrual of information about self and world. [For them] the only "real world" is that experienced in the "normal" waking phase and even the exploration of alternative phases is typically disparaged. . . . Within [these Western cultures] those engaging in the exploration of alternative states of consciousness, with or without the use of drugs, may be perceived by others as deviant, crazy, antisocial, evil, or criminally dangerous. (4–5)

In other words, the lack of understanding about alternative states of consciousness under which Twain labored is still with us, adding to the miseries of people (such as schizophrenics or epileptics) who experience them without their own volition and undermining any serious consideration of where the visions might come from or what they could mean. But for Indigenous Australians, altered states of consciousness are gateways into an alternative reality. Cathy Craigie describes it as living in more than one world. "We see this as 'normal,'" she told me. "We had 'clever' women and men who could talk to the natural world and the supernatural world. They could move between time and space and dimensions."[4] Not only could individuals shift between different dimensions of reality; they also did not bear the burden of Western conceptions of good and evil, gods and devils. As Hume explains it, in Aboriginal religions, even though "some myths have moral content, the idea of original sin and moral corruption is absent. Powerful spirits are present but there is no notion of a god or gods who have authority over all. There is no concept of reconcilement, and there is no heaven or hell, reward or punishment. Like human beings, Ancestors are both good and bad. The Dreaming Ancestors established both a pattern of relevancies and a moral order that extended to everything. Living people are connected metaphysically, geographically and in essence to each other and all other beings, places, and events in the Dreaming. Human beings live in a landscape that is 'saturated with significations,' and the shape and form of that landscape is living proof of those Dreaming events" (27).

All this sounds a lot like the kinds of issues Twain was tackling in his dream writings, his speculations about mental telepathy, and his quest to understand the sources of his creativity. The Aboriginal artist knows that his or her creations partake of eternal realities and, most importantly, that she or he is neither alone nor individually responsible. "In the western world people try to analyze and control instead of accepting that there are things that are beyond our control," Cathy Craigie notes. "I see this with nature. Western thinking sees nature as a commodity but Aboriginal people see it as connected and necessary to their own existence. Even totems were a way of preserving species and the environment. All aspects of Aboriginal life were connected to the spiritual world and the natural world." From this point of view Twain's nightmare writings could be a warning from the Ancestors that he was holding on too hard, that he had to recognize that the everyday world, the world he assumed to be real, was as fully ephemeral as the worlds he dreamed. If he could give up the material, including beloved family members and his own need for control, he would understand everyone's place in the vast network of the Ancestors, the dead, the living, and the yet to be born. He would also realize that he was a member of a community rather than a lone individual. Best of all, he would have no need to feel that the world's evil was a product of his own imagination. He almost got there on his own, but he didn't have either the vocabulary or the logics to follow it out. And so, as his late writings show us, he continued to struggle with his philosophical contemporaries, his guilt, and his God.

6

Staring at Animals

Mark Twain loved animals. He adored cats, respected dogs, and used both—along with birds, horses, and other creatures—as characters throughout his writings. Traveling gave him a chance to study animals in other countries, especially their adaptations to human cultures different from his own. So animals were definitely on my *Following* agenda. I like animals, too, and I looked forward to traveling with Mark Twain through the kingdom of exotic fauna—Australian kangaroos, Indian tigers, South African elephants. I figured this would be the fun part of my research.

It was fun—no question—but tough, beginning with the simple act of finding the animals. Twain had the same experience. The first thing he noticed about native Australian animals was that they weren't there. "We saw birds," he remembered, "but not a kangaroo, not an emu, not an ornithorhynchus, not a lecturer, not a native. Indeed, the land seemed quite destitute of game" (*FE* 155). For the record, "ornithorhynchus" is the Latin term for a platypus. A word lover, Twain embraced "ornithorhynchus" and used it whenever he could. I'll get back to the "game" reference in Twain's comment later, but right now I want to stick with his assessment of Australian wildlife. It turns out that all the way back in 1895, the only way Mark Twain could see native Australian mammals was to go to the Adelaide zoo. By the time he got there, he had begun ruminating on wildlife extermination. He had already encountered several laughing jackasses (a species of kingfisher, also known as kookaburras), and their presence in the zoo triggered his speculation on the longevity of the species. "In time man will exterminate the wild creatures of Australia, but this one will probably survive, for man is his friend and lets him alone," he mused. "Man always has a good reason for his charities towards wild things, human or animal—when he has any. In this case the bird is spared because he kills snakes. If L.J. will take my advice he will not kill all of them" (*FE* 185). He was less optimistic for the Australian dingo. Despite being "a beautiful creature—shapely, graceful, a little wolfish in some of his aspects, but with a most friendly eye and sociable disposition," the wild dog liked to raid sheep pens, and the settler farmers were out to get him. "He has been sentenced to extermination," Twain caustically observed. "This is all right, and not objectionable. The world was made for man—the white man" (*FE* 186).

"The world was made for man" is a reference to Francis Bacon's *Novum Organum*, a Utilitarian document that provided an easy rationale for imperialism in the name of progress. "The world was made for man . . . not man for the world," Bacon asserts. From this viewpoint, nature's only use value was utilitarian, a view that nineteenth-century settlers embraced because it justified eliminating any creature that got in their way. Twain's own gut instinct led him elsewhere; although he agreed with the Utilitarians' claim that people act only from self-interest, the idea didn't make him happy. At bottom, Samuel Clemens was a moralist, and his moralism struggled against his Utilitarianism for much of his life. Add to that his sympathy for animals, coupled with an instinctive aversion to waste, and you get a man for whom wantonly slaughtered animals—a favorite activity of the "sportsmen" of his era—represented the worst of human nature. In her introduction to *Mark Twain's Book of Animals* (2010), a collection of Twain's animal sketches, Shelley Fisher Fishkin notes that Twain traced his aversion to hunting to a boyhood experience of killing a bird in the midst of song. After the bird fell lifeless at his feet young Clemens realized the consequences of his impulsive shot: "I had not needed that harmless creature," Twain remembers, "I had destroyed it wantonly, and I felt all that an assassin feels, of grief and remorse when his deed comes home to him and he wishes he could undo it and have his hands and his soul clean again from accusing blood" (Fisher Fishkin 3). Eventually Twain's sentiments extended to the popular sport of hunting: William Dean Howells, one of his closest friends, noted that Twain "abhorred the dull and savage joy of the sportsman" (Fisher Fishkin 3).

So by the time he arrived in Australia, Twain was fully conversant not just with settler rationales for species elimination but also with hunter rationales for their sport, and his comment about what he did *not* see on the Australian landscape resonates with both. I'm neither a hunter nor a settler, and although I am certainly conscious of my own generation's conversations about both hunting (I lived ten years in State College, Pennsylvania, smack in the middle of vast tracts of game preserves) and species extinction, I wasn't sure how to bring Twain's observations about the disappearance of indigenous fauna up to date. I started with a handful of undigested assumptions that almost all turned out to be false. I knew that despite the horrific pace of species annihilation throughout the twentieth century, the environmental movement had brought animal conservation to the forefront of public consciousness. My sense was that more and more countries were recognizing that extermination of inconvenient plants and animals precipitates ecological disaster, and that they were beginning to find means of preserving the wild. I also assumed that most animal conservation venues would be run either by government agencies or by nonprofit organizations specifically focused on conservation issues—like the Nature Conservancy in the United States. I was right about public consciousness, but not about who runs what show there is. As Twain observed, the eighteenth through early twentieth centuries were all about colonial expansion and its concomitant: getting rid of animal, vegetable, and human species that stood in the way. We know the outcome: thousands of animal and plant species gone extinct, and thousands more on the brink. Now a great deal of money and energy is being devoted to figuring out how to preserve those species that remain. It's not just a conversation among scientists, either: "how" includes "by whom" and "for whom." I had to learn to ask those questions, and doing so tumbled me into the economics of ecotourism. They taught me something about the history of animal refuges in the West, and they also forced me to think about how my own desire to look at exotic animals plays into the industry of wildlife conservation.

Very few people were thinking about conservation when Twain traipsed through the British Empire. Rather the opposite—the European settlers who were reshaping the globe were not only slaughtering native species but also importing plants and animals that crowded out the indigenes that remained. Twain remarks on the havoc wreaked on ecosystems (he didn't use that word) in Australia and New Zealand by the importation of rabbits. "The man who introduced the rabbit [to New Zealand] was banqueted and lauded; but they would hang him, now, if they could get him," he observes (FE 285). Since then, species extinction has reached crisis proportions, but there is no consensus about how to deal with it. International agencies publish guidelines and individual countries pass piecemeal legislation, but there is little oversight, and paltry punishment for infractions. In lieu of effective global government policies, business—very big business—has stepped into the breach. In retrospect I realize that Twain's bitter observation that "the world was made for man—the white man" goes directly to the heart of the debates about how and why we should care about animal conservation, and about who gets to be in charge of the conversation. Even more presciently, his comments about what he could *not* see suggest the extent to which seeing—*looking at*—has become a driving force in the business of creating wildlife sanctuaries. I started my journeys assuming that most wildlife sanctuaries exist to repair the ecosystems of the world. By the end

I realized that most exist to make profits for their investors by feeding tourists' desire to see the exotic. Even sanctuaries that do seek to maintain or rebuild the wild cannot function without funding, and the people who fork over money for animal preservation want to see what they are supporting. Hence all wildlife conservation centers rely on human curiosity, the desire to stare at anything new. As Twain understood, animals and Indigenous peoples have become, like "lecturers," entertainment for a mass consumer audience.

It took me a long time to understand this. I not only had to do the traveling but also had to learn how to think about animal venues, their histories, ownerships, and missions, and later, to teach myself something about the history of hunting and of conservation theory and to read the literature about animals and the human gaze. Learning how to think about animal conservation was part of my learning how to rethink my project. The methodology I evolved for the animal section was pretty simple. I came as a tourist, eager to see what the venue offered, taking notes on what I saw and how I felt about it, and watching the people around me. Later, I asked my questions about ownership, goals, and accomplishments. When I got home I started the serious background research: the websites listing international ownership (thank you, colleagues in the KU Business School), ecology literature, philosophical essays on the gaze. The method proved surprisingly productive. Because I gave free rein to my tourist impulses, I quickly caught on to the centrality of human visual desire to all the animal sites, no matter what their organizational structure. Twain's complaint about not seeing what he expected to see first alerted me to the issue, but my own pleasure in seeing what I did see forced me to recognize it as the linchpin of animal conservation venues worldwide.

I'm not the first person to note that people like to stare at animals. Perhaps the best known of the many essays on this topic is John Berger's 1977 "Why Look at Animals?" from his collection *About Looking*. Berger argues that beginning in the nineteenth century, the Western world has progressively marginalized animals, until even ordinary farm animals have become exotic (think petting zoos). I am seeing a further evolution: first the exotic was transformed into consumer spectacle, then the spectacular was enlisted in the work of animal conservation. Now, as the director of the Phillip Island Penguin Foundation told me, most wild animal refuges fund their projects by foregrounding the spectacular.

In Twain's time, the exotic was the major draw, along with a vigorous public relations campaign to sell "nature" to an increasingly urban population. Twain himself, perhaps unwittingly, was part of the public relations framework: his own writings about the uncultivated, unbuilt environment suggested that city dwellers could enjoy traveling through these spaces. Works like *Roughing It* (1872), which contained lyrical descriptions of the American West and Hawaii, gave the impression that touring the wilderness was a relatively easy venture. One of his best-known maxims, "nothing helps scenery like ham and eggs" (*Roughing It* 117), suggested that traveling could be a pleasant and leisurely pursuit. But not everyone could travel. Zoos, too, proliferated during this period. Wealthy families had kept private zoos for many years, but the modern zoo evolved from the same impulse that created nature tourism. For those city dwellers whose income or tastes precluded a camping trip in the wilderness, a visit to the local zoo could have educational and recreational benefits with no discomfort at all. There they could stare at exotic animals as long as they wanted and then head home to dinner and comfortable beds.

The other big strategy for selling nature to Americans focused, ironically, on killing its denizens. In *Hunting and the American Imagination* (2001), Daniel Justin Herman traces the history of the idea that "Americans are (or were) a hunting people and that it was hunting that made them American" (x). According to this particularly male-oriented narrative of American identity, if the wildlife disappeared, so too would the manly pursuit of hunting, and with it, the virtues of American masculinity. Hence the movement to dedicate large sections of the public domain to the maintenance of the American wilderness. President Theodore Roosevelt, who brought the US government into the business of saving the wilderness for hunters, was, in the long run, also the most powerful force behind saving the animals themselves (Herman 12).

Happily, none of this was on my mind when I started my travels. I just wanted to see the animals. I started looking for kangaroos on the runway as my plane landed in Sydney. (In self-defense let me say that I have seen coyotes on airport runways in Kansas.) No luck there, but I did get a few glimpses out in the country. I have friends in Melbourne, Rob and Sue Pascoe, fantastic hosts and informants. Rob took me on a long day's tour of the small towns Twain visited outside Melbourne, and that's when I spotted my first kangaroos. I would have missed the troop if Rob hadn't called my attention to it. We were driving through an upscale country neighborhood, the kind where private homes are embedded in four to five acres of lightly tended woodlands. Rob pointed to a group of three large kangaroos in a small clearing. I grabbed my camera and leaped out of the car; the kangaroos took one frightened look at me and bounded off. My photographs were so fuzzy I ended up deleting them. My second sighting was the same day, and more memorable. Dusk, on a high-speed highway, Rob driving, a hands-free cell phone device glued to his head. Rob is a nervous, high-energy talker, and he is giving a rapid-fire interview to a Melbourne paper about a book on football he is writing. Looking past him at the highway's shoulder I see a kangaroo posed atop a berm, silhouetted against the darkening sky. No time to even raise my camera, but the picture will stay in my mind forever.

These days, kangaroos are protected under Australian law, which means there are more of them around than in Twain's time. The law isn't universally popular—Aussie farmers don't like kangaroos because they compete with domestic animals for grazing grounds. "Farmers shoot them when they think they can get away with it," Rob commented. Hence kangaroos live nervously, springing away from humans. But not always. Sue told me one story about a wallaby encounter that spoke directly to my interest in the gaze. Wallabies are smaller cousins of kangaroos, and many live in the bush on Phillip Island, where Sue and Rob own a beach house that backs onto the low, dense, foliage. Sue's encounter happened at dusk, the hour when wallabies begin to roam. She was hanging clothes to dry outside, standing on a concrete platform that extends from the back of the house into the yard. Suddenly aware she was being watched, she looked up and into the eyes of a wallaby staring at her from the platform's edge. "It was an intense moment," she told me. "Really weird. We were staring into each other's eyes, in some way communicating across species. I felt the hairs on my neck curl."

Sue's encounter was unusual. Australia's indigenous animals may be more plentiful than they used to be, but few are willing to let themselves be examined up close—especially, it seems, by a curious American. I not only had trouble sighting kangaroos; even the cockatoos screaming from the treetops in Sydney scattered if I leaned out my hotel window. Frustrated in my desire to see up close and familiar, I followed Twain's lead and went to a zoo. In Sydney I spent a happy couple of hours at the Wild Life Sydney Zoo, which focuses on indigenous fauna.[1] It is owned by Merlin Entertainments, a British company that also owns Legoland, Madame Tussauds, and Cypress Gardens. Dubai International Capital, a branch of the Dubai ruling family's investment holdings, was for a time a 20 percent shareholder. The zoo's public face is all about protecting indigenous fauna, but it's pretty clear that profits are its real motive. One of the lessons I've learned during this process concerns the

"Protection Narrative"—a term I'm using to describe the story commercial venues use to convince visitors that the hefty entrance fees they pay to see exotic animals are helping the animals survive. This narrative also has its roots in the nineteenth century, in precisely the kind of animal decimation that Twain describes in his passage about the Adelaide zoo. In addition to providing recreation for local families, nineteenth-century "zoological gardens" were sites for scientific study of animal physiology and behavior, especially of animals about to disappear from the earth—a mission that has continued to today. By the late twentieth century, as the world began to wake up to the consequences of species extinction, "protection" became one of the rationales for continuing to keep wild animals in captivity; now zoos can argue that their mission is to protect endangered species by providing safe spaces for individuals to live and breed. Under attack by critics who contend that animals bred in captivity are not the same as those born in the wild (not to mention that some species simply do not reproduce in captivity), the rationale nevertheless provides an effective marketing tool for animal venues that need public support to keep themselves financially viable. Hence the "Protection Narrative," which often operates through the labels next to the exhibits. For instance, at the Wild Life Sydney Zoo the label for the Tasmanian devil, a small marsupial, told us that the species is suffering from devil facial tumor disease, a contagious cancer. Hence, the label implies, this was a rescue animal, being isolated from contagion in the hopes that he (or she) will help rebuild the population. A feel-good story for well-meaning humans, but not so great for the Tasmanian devil. As far as I could see, this animal was living in a marsupial's hell. The small enclosure was glassed in, providing few hiding places, and he circled the small space incessantly, clearly looking for respite from the peering, chattering humans who surrounded his pen.

Peering and chattering characterize the crowds that flock to the Wild Life Sydney Zoo—and I was one of them. Billy didn't come with me on my first pass through Australia, so I didn't have a companion to chatter to. Instead I chattered to the families around me—many of whom were South Asians who were clearly fascinated by the Australian fauna they were seeing. We chattered and we posed, swapping cell phones so we could get snapshots of ourselves up against the enclosures. In an eerie echo of the history of sportsmen's clubs, which celebrate successful hunts by photographing the hunters posing with their dead prey, the zoo offers visitors the opportunity to have their picture taken holding a (live) koala, if they pay extra. I was actually planning to pay my money and get the picture—I thought it would make a great publicity poster. This, by the way, may have been the moment I first started noticing my complicity in the wildlife business. Selfies are not really my thing. Any of my family members will tell you how hard it is to get me to pose for a picture. Yet here I was willing to lay down cash for a picture of me with a captive animal—a picture I'd be using to advertise myself. What was I thinking? In the end, I didn't have the photo taken because the koala was asleep, and a napping koala didn't seem particularly engaging. FYI: koalas sleep all the time. Rob told me it is because they eat eucalyptus leaves, which contain a soporific. I don't know whether that's true, but the bottom line is that as spectacle, koalas are boring. They are imperiled, though, in part because so many are killed by cars as they lumber across roads. Others are destroyed by dogs, and even more die from habitat decimation. So there is a need to protect them.

"Using captive koalas as a photo op can't be the best protection strategy," I told myself when I turned down the offer. Once I started reading about the history of animal conservation, though, I realized that it's a fairly effective one. Having your picture taken with a live animal is the flip side of those photographs of hunters surrounded by dead animals—a genre arguably more popular at the turn of the twentieth century than it is today, but still alive and well.[2] Photographs are not only documents about the past; they are also spectacle. As an art, photography is all about "staring at"—looking at a scene of a place and time where, at the moment you are looking at the photograph, you are not. If I had had the photo taken, I would have been able to (a) prove that I had been there (the documentary aspect), and (b) show that the zoo had given me the rare privilege of cuddling a live koala (the spectacular aspect), potentially bringing yet more customers to the venue. The upshot would have been a certain amount of cachet for me, and, as my viewers sought similar experiences, more revenue for the zoo.

I freely admit that I enjoyed my hours at the Wild Life Sydney Zoo. I even liked the insects. The conservation literature tells us that it's a lot harder to get people excited about insects than about tigers and kangaroos, but the zoo does a nice job with spiders. I wished Twain had had a chance to see the golden orb-weaver, a spider that weaves a golden web. He could have spun infinite metaphors from it. And I loved the butterfly room, where I stood—no glass windows here—surrounded by fluttering swatches of color.

Still, by the end of the day I was also asking whether this zoo's mission is really to protect animals, or whether that is just a cynical manipulation of popular conservation sentiment for commercial ends. If the people who run the Wild Life Sydney Zoo really care about animal rescue and protection, why is the Tasmanian devil in such a cruel enclosure? Devils are nocturnal creatures who burrow away from the light and prefer habitats of forest and scrub brush. Was the devil I saw on display because the authorities knew its carnivorous reputation would draw a crowd? Was it being sacrificed for the greater good of the species? An article on the fate of research chimpanzees in the *New York Times* in 2015 notes that under the Endangered Species Act, animals can be used for research only if the research benefits the species as a whole (Gormer). According to Mark A. Michel, editor of *Preserving Wildlife: An International Perspective*, the Utilitarian view of conservation is a form of free-market economics, which argues that turning individuals into commodities is moral as long as the ends justify the means (15). In this reading the Tasmanian devil's misery was all for the greater good of its species—provided the zoo's profits go to maintain them. I am not sure that happens at this venue. The zoo's ownership by an international conglomerate suggests that the profits leave Australia's borders—and devils don't exist outside Australia. Despite the pleasure I had that afternoon, I was forced to realize that the zoo's animals are commodities pure and simple, on display for a public willing to pay a hefty fee for the privilege of peering at the exotic from behind a glass wall. The "for whom" answer here was "Merlin Entertainments' investors." Moreover, my happy participation in the peering and chattering also led me to formulate that second research question: What does my role as a consumer of animal spectacle mean in the landscape of animal conservation strategies worldwide?

It took a visit to a very different kind of wildlife refuge (and a lot of later research) to begin to find out. From Australia I skip to South Africa, and to Nkomazi, a small, privately owned animal reserve about three and a half hours' drive east of Johannesburg. Time constraints forced me to fly between Durban and Johannesburg, so a road trip from Johannesburg to Nkomazi was a welcome chance to see something of the South African countryside, especially the veld. Twain himself traveled by train throughout South Africa, recording his admiration for the landscape in his journal. On a trip from Johannesburg to Bloemfontein in late May 1896, he noted, "I think the veld in its sober winter garb is as beautiful as Paradise. There were unlevel stretches, day before yesterday, where it went rolling & swelling, & rising & subsiding, & sweeping grandly on & on, & still on & on, like an ocean, toward the remote horizon, its pale brown deepening by delicately graduated shades to rich orange, & finally to purple & crimson where it washed against the wooded hills & naked red crags at the base of the sky."[3] Twain loved ocean vistas; their endless billows represented release from social pressures to him, so for him to compare a landscape to the ocean was high praise. Despite his descriptions of the scenery, however, Twain makes almost no mention of animals in the South Africa portion of *Following the Equator*, so they weren't on my original agenda. However, the KU colleagues helping me plan my South Africa sojourn convinced me that I shouldn't leave the country without visiting a wildlife preserve. It didn't take much persuasion. I had wanted to visit an African preserve ever since cousin Marj enthused about the ones she had visited in Botswana and South Africa, so I sifted through the venues my colleagues suggested and made a reservation at Nkomazi. I had no idea how central it would become to my thinking about wildlife conservation values. It also helped me think through some of Twain's own commentary about settler-led campaigns for species annihilation, and about the hunters whose fear that the sport (and their masculinity) would die with the demise of the wilderness initiated the first wildlife conservation projects.

In terms of spectacle Nkomazi wins hands down. I loved every second of my time there. It is beautifully run, with informed guides, luxury accommodations, plentiful wildlife, and stunning scenery. "Improving scenery with ham and eggs," indeed! Try multicourse dinners and South African wines. Billy and I spent two and a half days there, going on three-hour guided drives mornings and evenings and lounging in or near our luxury tent the rest of the time, listening to the sound of the nearby river. I discovered (who knew?) that I loved getting up at 4:00 A.M., sipping tea while watching the African sun etch itself above the opposite hill. And I fell in love with the young cheetah brothers who roamed the reserve, teaching themselves to hunt. I'm happy to give Nkomazi a tourist thumbs up: this is a great place to take a vacation.

Unfortunately, I couldn't just indulge my spectacle cravings at Nkomazi—I was supposed to be doing research. So I started asking my questions about ownership, beginning with the "by whom/for whom" question. "It's owned by Dubai World Africa," our guide informed me. "Read the information packet in your tent," another guest advised. "The company bought it for two reasons," the guide added, "because they were looking to diversify from oil, and because they want to 'give back' to the land."

Seriously? Dubai wants to "give back" to South Africa? I doubted it. Even I'm not *that* naïve. I could see why Dubai might think it wise to diversify from oil, but I was dubious about the "giving back" line. If Dubai wanted to "give back" to the environment, how about starting with the devastation its growth has inflicted on its own ecosystems? Remembering that Dubai International Capital had been heavily invested in Merlin Entertainments, which owns the Wild Life Sydney Zoo, I wanted to know exactly who owned Dubai World Africa. Two weeks into my South Africa sojourn I had already learned that stunning landscapes and exotic animals aren't the country's only riches: beneath them are treasures in gold, platinum, diamonds, coal, magnesium, and other resources. I wondered whether land ownership in South Africa included mineral rights. I went back to my tent and read the packet, which did indeed frame Dubai World Africa's investment within conservation principles. The "story of Nkomazi Game Reserve," the packet page records, "began nearly a decade ago. Laying the foundations for one of the most extraordinary initiatives in Africa, the artificial structures and redundant infrastructures were removed from the farms. The rehabilitation of agricultural and other disturbed land began and wildlife was introduced to a 6500 hectare specially fenced area. Dubai World Africa's investment in this African dream will see it becoming a reality and being shared with thousands of South Africans and visitors to the country." The info sheet also quotes DWA's chair, Sultan Ahmed bin Sulayem, as saying, "I am confident that the company will emerge as the best example for ensuring sustainable investments that are economically viable and at the same time environmentally enriching for Africa." It was the best-written example of the Protection Narrative I'd run into so far.

There were no dates included in the tent packet, and a Google search revealed that Sultan bin Sulayem has not chaired Dubai World Africa since late 2010. Finding out who does—or more relevantly, who oversees Nkomazi—is not easy, at least through ordinary internet searches. Like Dubai International Capital, Dubai World Africa is an investment arm of the Dubai government, and in 2008 the Competition Tribunal of South Africa approved Dubai World Africa's acquisition of a majority share in three South African game reserves, all developed by Adrian Gardiner, an energetic and far-sighted entrepreneur. There were holding companies involved here—it's a complex game—but my research confirmed that in 2014, the year I visited, Dubai World Africa did indeed own Nkomazi, along with at least two other South African wildlife reserves.

Perhaps the most productive way to think about Nkomazi is within the global development of wildlife reserves from Twain's time to ours—in itself a kind of historical take on the "by whom/for whom" question.

This approach also introduces a "winners/losers" element that the Wild Life Sydney Zoo obscured. At reserves like Nkomazi, the human winners are the white South Africans and the foreign entrepreneurs, and the losers are the folks who lived there before the whites arrived. The growth of Kruger National Park is a prime example. South African wildlife venues began as private hunting preserves for the white elite, who kicked both Indigenous peoples and poorer white settlers off parcels of land to create a white fantasy about the African wild (think Ernest Hemingway). In the 1920s, under the rubric of conservation, some of the private reserves were consolidated and nationalized, eventually becoming Kruger. Successive apartheid governments managed to keep it and its facilities as a whites-only enclave until the late 1980s. Roughly the size of Connecticut, Kruger is now open to all: at a garden party in Pretoria we listened to multiracial families discussing their plans for Christmas holidays in the park.

Clearly Kruger sprang from Utilitarian values. The animals were saved because a powerful human group—white hunters—decided they were useful. As such, Kruger is part of the modern history of game preserves, a story about the development of national parks and the animal refuges that evolved from them that is as widespread and as systematic as the "final solution" to Indigenous peoples. It was a history with which Twain was personally familiar, in part as a consequence of his own youthful sojourns in the American West, in part as a consequence of his friendship with wealthy eastern families who maintained private hunting "camps" in the Adirondacks, and in part through his contentious relationship with then-president Theodore Roosevelt, who represented both the pluses and minuses of animal conservation for much of the United States.

The "discovery" of nature as an antidote to the stresses and diseases of the crowded city had begun during Twain's youth. Springing up primarily among the inhabitants of the Eastern Seaboard, it was a movement to restore both physical and spiritual health through periodic immersion in nature. It was also associated with the Romantic school of painting, itself with ties to German nature painting. Twain and Livy's friend Frederic Edwin Church was one of the leading American Romantic painters, and Twain and Livy visited Church's Hudson Valley home, Olana, a house built to maximize views over the gardens, river valley, and hills beyond. Popular before the evolution of landscape photography, in the mid-nineteenth century such paintings served the spectacular ends of the emerging cult of nature, especially in large canvases like Church's meticulously detailed *Heart of the Andes* and Albert Bierstadt's

A Storm in the Rocky Mountains.[4] But nature as Church and Bierstadt portrayed it was disappearing even as they painted it, and the pressure was mounting to preserve some of it for posterity. The most effective push for wild animal reserves came not from esthetes but from white hunters, who witnessed the erosion of the animals' habitats as white "civilization" spread across the United States in the latter part of the nineteenth century. As John F. Reiger argued in *American Sportsmen and the Origins of Conservation* (1975), "American sportsmen, those who hunted and fished for pleasure rather than commerce or necessity, were the real spearhead of conservation" (21). Theodore Roosevelt, whose love of the hunt was the target of more than one of Twain's barbed commentaries, became famous for creating the nation's parks precisely to preserve hunting and hunting culture. In *Shapers of the Great Debate on Conservation: A Biographical Dictionary* (2004), Rachel White Scheuering records that during Roosevelt's presidency he created "230 million acres of protected areas in the form of 18 national monuments, 5 national parks, 51 national wildlife refuges, and 150 national forests" (xix), all with the idea that they would preserve the "strenuous life" that wilderness hunting represented for the American male (and occasional female).

Where does Mark Twain fit into all this? Both within and without, I think. Twain's life coincided with the evolution of the cult of nature and the evolution of American hunting culture, and he evolved along with them, from eagerly joining "coon hunts" as a boy to recording hunting parties during his California and Nevada years, to satirizing hunting mythology from at least the 1890s on. If true, his anecdote about realizing that in impulsively shooting a bird he had taken an "innocent" life on a whim suggests that his attitude toward hunting as sport (not the same as hunting for food) began to shift during his adolescence. What we know is that by the 1890s he had come a long way. Possibly influenced by the women in his family, who were all members of early forms of the Society for the Prevention of Cruelty to Animals, and certainly out of his affection for and sense of kinship with the animal world, Twain became publicly as well as emotionally opposed to killing as sport. Teddy Roosevelt, whose *Good Hunting: In Pursuit of Big Game in the West* (1907) Twain owned and marked (Gribben 2:587), was one of his favorite targets simply because the president was such a conspicuous advocate of the pastime. In "The President Hunts a Cow," an autobiographical dictation from October 21, 1907, Twain lambasted Roosevelt's "dime-novel" adventures chasing wildlife and his participation in the self-justifying belief that killing animals was a "sport," with rules that both humans and the animals themselves understood (*Autobiography of Mark Twain*, 3:174–76). The headlines reporting Roosevelt's adventures, accompanied by ample photographs of the man with his kill, only proved that the president was into it for the attention it brought him. "He takes a boy's delight in showing off," Twain averred (175). Spectacular indeed.

If we add these moments of personal history to Twain's latter-day observation that many species were being driven to extinction by the onslaught of western settlers, it seems reasonable to assume that Mark Twain would have approved of wildlife refuges founded to preserve, rather than kill, wild animals—though he, like me, might have harbored some doubts about their rationales. Nkomazi is the sort of place the Clemenses would have visited in South Africa, had it existed in 1896; throughout his lecture tour, Twain's hosts routinely treated the family to the special sights of their regions. Nkomazi represents a new form of wildlife refuge, one the antihunting Clemens family would have enjoyed. Established much later than Yosemite or Kruger, it was never a hunting preserve. Moreover, its narrative suggests that its raison d'être was not only to preserve wildlife, but to do so for wildlife's own sake, rather than as a means of entertaining humans. From the first, it was part of the ecotourism movement that began in the late twentieth century and that Adrian Gardiner saw as an exciting business venture. In the 1990s Gardiner began by buying up "degraded" farmlands, meaning farms made unprofitable through drought, overgrazing, invasive species, and absentee landlordism. One of the first entrepreneurs in South Africa to see such lands as suitable for the process called "rewilding," he discovered that the process wasn't as easy as he originally thought. His farmer neighbors resisted fiercely. Their grandparents had fought to eradicate predatory beasts, and they did not want to see them reintroduced. Learning the sequencing for species introduction was also a trial and error process. Gardiner introduced wild dogs too early in the sequence, and they ate all the other animals. "They were the prime predator," he remembers. "They would pick a species; wipe out that species and then move on to the next easiest one to catch" (Sevier). In the end, though, Gardiner created a model for rewilding—one so successful that Dubai World Africa bought a majority share. Now ecotourism, as at Nkomazi, is a major South African industry.

I think South Africa is especially interesting because it exhibits tensions between animal and human groups that exist elsewhere but tend to be less pronounced. As Twain observed, conservation isn't only about animals. It's about who gets to use the land, and how. When Roosevelt established Yosemite National Park, Native Americans who had always lived there were expelled. The same process happened in South Africa. When Adrian Gardiner claims that the farms he bought up were unprofitable, he is referring to the Lockean argument that land belongs only to those who can make it yield. But the same logic had been used by the white farmers when they appropriated the land from Indigenous Africans, who can now argue that the farmlands were never really the whites' to sell. In situations like this governments have a choice: give the land to someone who will enter it into the market system, or return it to the people who have a historical claim to it but who may not choose to make it profitable. By and large South Africa has chosen the former, arguing, as does Gardiner, that enterprises like the reserves provide jobs for locals in an otherwise job-poor region.

And I think they do—give employment to the locals, that is. Most of the staff I spoke to at Nkomazi came from the region: Bianca, our guide, from farm country about two hours distant; my masseuse from the nearby town of Badplaas; the serving staff also from the area. All this sounds great until you look at the color hierarchy, beginning with the chorus of black staff members who sing you greetings at the entrance. This probably doesn't bother most visitors, and it certainly would not have bothered Twain, for whom the sight of black South Africans frequently (and pleasurably) reminded him of the African Americans of his Missouri boyhood. It definitely bothered Billy and me. The smiling, singing faces reminded us both way too much of "happy darky" stereotypes of our American childhoods. But the singers were our introduction to the social structure we would observe over the next three days, so they jumpstarted our learning curve. At Nkomazi the color hierarchy works in tandem with the employment hierarchy: the guides, at the top of the visible heap, are both white Afrikaners; the managers of the spa are white; the range managers are white; and everyone else—cooks, servers, workers out on the land—are black. On the invisible side, Dubai, an Arab state, owns the reserve, and Dubai World Africa's then-CEO, James Wilson, is white. So the whole question of "by whom/for whom" is immensely complicated here. In the hierarchy of humans who work the place, Nkomazi hasn't come very far from the days of apartheid. In terms of environmental consciousness, on the other hand, it seems to do a pretty good job. As far as I can tell, Nkomazi is about as ecologically conscious as a high-end tourist venue can hope to be—meaning that despite having to install toilets, showers, plunge pools, electricity, and refrigeration, it is trying to leave as light a human footprint as possible. One response to this is that it's easy to be ecologically responsible if you are rich—which of course explains Nkomazi's origins as an ecotourism venue. It's not as expensive as a lot of the South African reserves we considered, but it is definitely not cheap. As for the wildlife, it's clear that Nkomazi is trying to manage the animals "naturally"—meaning it creates as native a habitat as possible and is mindful of the animals' welfare, otherwise leaving them alone.

Nkomazi features many bodily pleasures beyond the visual, including private plunge pools, good South African wine, and a spa—not strong inducements to research rigor. This is living with the wild in the most luxurious way possible. For me the fantasy worked until the morning we topped a hill overlooking the surrounding countryside. From there I spotted the fence that separates the reserve from the roads, farms, and villages on the other side. I looked at it and realized how willingly I had engaged in Nkomazi's elaborate game of "let's pretend." I had not only pretended I was a tourist of the luxury class but had believed the guides when they implied that the reserve's foremost objective was the animals' welfare. On the contrary. As Twain was well aware, the wildlife was all part of the "game"—pun intended—for curious visitors. The real objective was getting me to spend my money at Nkomazi; the animals are well cared for because the managers know that they are the entertainment that will open my wallet.

Nkomazi looms large in my conservation education, the place where my earlier questioning of my own motives became central to my project. I was getting a real kick out of these sites, not to speak of lolling in high-end touristic pleasures. I could tell myself that the money I was spending was helping preserve the animals, but that was just the problem. If the tourists disappear, what happens to the creatures? I don't for a minute believe that Dubai World Africa would maintain Nkomazi in the absence of profits, no matter what the promotional literature claims. The animals' welfare was dependent on the continuation of my gaze, my desire—my budget. I can hear Twain's acerbic commentary now. And he would be right: Is this a sustainable strategy for wildlife preservation?

I felt a little more encouraged after I talked with an actual conservator. My last conservation location was in Australia, at the little penguin sanctuary on Phillip Island, off the Melbourne coast. Again, this visit is indebted to Rob and Sue. Despite years of taking children and grandchildren to see the little (or "fairy") penguins, Rob remains enamored of them, and he happily took me to the evening show, where we sat cooing as the penguins scurried past us. Like Nkomazi, this is an outdoor venue, in this case on the beach, with viewing stands on the margins between the beach proper and the dunes where the birds dig their burrows. In the mornings the penguins head out to the water, where they spend the entire day fishing, traveling up to fifty kilometers per day. They return at dusk, rushing up the beach in groups to avoid predators—but directly in the sights of the stadium-style seats lining their paths. You would think that after a day fishing in the Bass Strait they would be exhausted, but not so.[5] Instead of crashing, they spend the night cruising up and down the streets of their villages, volubly demonstrating their considerable vocabulary of shrills, trills, squeaks, and shrieks. It's like, check in with the missus and the chick, then waddle off to the pub for a pint and a good time. They are really cute and really funny—which puts them in the "spectacular" camp. They are also really protected, which brings us back to the "by whom/for whom" question.

Like Nkomazi, the little penguin sanctuary is situated on pre-viously settled land. Phillip Island is very near Melbourne, and by the mid-twentieth century, it was fairly densely settled. The penguin display (billed as the Penguin Parade) was run by commercial ventures purely for profit. Then the Victoria state government—not entrepreneurs—stepped in and began reversing the trend. As in the rewilding process at Nkomazi, they removed the human-made structures and returned the area to some-thing approaching the penguins' natural habitat—I say "approaching" because although they removed private residences (including Summer-land, an entire community), they also built viewing stands, boardwalks, a reception building (with gift shop and café), and huge parking lots to accommodate visitors. Now the penguin reserve is owned by the state of Victoria but run by Phillip Island Nature Parks, an organization to which the state has delegated care of the island's natural resources. In addition to the Penguin Parade, P. I. Nature Parks also controls the Koala Conser-vation Centre; The Nobbies, from which visitors can watch a seal colony; and the Churchill Island Heritage Farm, an annex of Phillip Island. The parks organization funnels its profits through the Penguin Foundation, which uses them for conservation and research.

The "by whom/for whom" question here seems fairly transparent. Research manager Peter Dann, who has been working with the little penguin colony since the 1980s, told me that funding for the scientific research comes from a combination of tourist and corporate dollars, with occasional contracts with local governments. The corporate money isn't grants. "Corporations fund projects that interest them," Dann told me. "They usually come to us because they hear about our research agen-das."[6] Exxon, for instance, contracted with the foundation on a system for tracking penguins out at sea, whereas Google engaged with a search for new methods for cleaning wildlife that had been contaminated by oil spills—the latter an issue, Dann noted drily, "we could never get oil companies excited about." At bottom is the corporations' self-interest: not only might the oceanographers' results play into some of the corporations' own research agendas, but the corporations reap valuable public relations benefits from claims that they support conservation research.

Talking with Peter Dann helped ease my discomfort about ecotourism. "Ecotourism takes many forms," he noted. "The little penguins are a good example." With six hundred thousand visitors annually, not only is the Penguin Parade worth AUD$400 million per year to the Victoria state economy, but the penguins are formative for local residents' regional identity. "The penguins are a part of the fabric of life in Victoria," Dann commented. Residents of the state come to Phillip Island when they are children, and like Rob, they bring their own children, and grandchildren, when they grow up. The programs encourage the locals to be proud of their natural heritage and to continue to support conservation efforts.

Locals aren't the only important target audience. As at the Wild Life Sydney Zoo, I noticed that many Chinese and South Asians populated the stands at the Penguin Parade. Rob told me that most arrive in the huge tourist buses we saw in the parking lot, coming down from Melbourne for the event and leaving immediately after. Peter Dann sees the parade as an important educational tool worldwide. "Many of the international visitors don't have access to information about conservation," Dann pointed out. The parks program piques their curiosity; they head home with questions about their own country's native fauna and conservation programs. And proximity to the penguins is a major factor. "It's hard to get people engaged in something they can't see and never will," Dann observed. "The parade makes the bond." Being there, watching the little birds scurry up the beach and trudge through the streets of their penguin "village," is a good way to help humans connect with the animals.

It sure worked with me. Dann's comments reaffirmed my realization that finding solutions to wildlife decimation hangs on the public—on me, my gaze, my curiosity. Although corporate and government contracts are significant, they cannot be relied on as a steady funding source. The public, on the other hand, provides a continuous income stream. That explains the consumerist pitch to the Nature Parks website. Overall, the message is that Phillip Island is a fun, family-friendly place to visit, a place for both active (the beaches are stunning, and the surf challenging) and passive (watching little penguins) engagement. All while educating the kids about conservation and contributing to it yourself with your dollars. What's not to like?

I think that what disturbs me about ecotourism is that for all the good work done by serious conservation projects like the Penguin Foundation and Phillip Island Nature Parks, the dependence of more and more of the earth's creatures on such arrangements indicates an alarming extension of human power over the wild. A popular theory among current earth scientists argues that the earth has entered a new epoch, dubbed the Anthropocene, in which human activity has irrevocably affected the entire environment, including climate and ecology. One solution to the devastation of the nonhuman world that accompanies massive human encroachment is to learn to "live with" the wild, as Jamie Lorimer, author of *Wildlife in the Anthropocene: Conservation after Nature*, puts it. But living with the wild has its drawbacks. Animals accustomed to human beings are not afraid to encroach on human space. Most Americans I know who live on the outskirts of small towns complain about deer devastating their gardens, and I rail at the squirrels who vandalize mine in Brooklyn. After I watched a small herd of Nkomazi elephants take down five trees in less than an hour, I realized how little we have to complain about. As for predatory beasts, a Kansas friend once told a hilarious story about his efforts to invent a coyote-proof chicken coop (he failed), but even his story paled beside a recent report of lions escaping from reserves near Nairobi and tigers from woodlands near Mumbai, posing serious threats to both domestic animals and humans.

Most Westerners have grown up under systems that segregate animals into specific spatial arenas—sheep, goats, cows, and horses in fields and barns; dogs and cats in and around houses; buffalo on the range; elephants in circuses, zoos, and wildlife sanctuaries. Animal segregation in the United States has become normative, leading to great consternation when animals cross boundaries and "invade" a differently designated space, like the coyotes that are periodically sighted in New York City's outlying parks, or the black bears that occasionally showed up in our suburban backyard when we lived in central Pennsylvania. Not only is the wild kept away from us; we are also kept away from it. For most of us, a visit to a zoo or a walk through a national park is the closest we are going to get to our region's native species.

That's why Sue's wallaby story is so eerie. Standing on the concrete platform outside her house, hanging clothes, Sue was contained within human space. The wallaby's encroachment on that space turned species privilege on her. Suddenly Sue was the object of the gaze: standing on a stage, performing human activities for the wallaby's amusement. When she looked at him, he looked back. We do not expect wild animals to meet our eyes, much less to stroll over to stare at us. That is our human prerogative.

So I come back to Mark Twain's observation that he saw neither a kangaroo, nor an emu, nor an ornithorhyncus, "not a lecturer, not a native. Indeed, the land seemed quite destitute of game," and to his bitter recognition that human beings will eliminate anything not immediately useful to them. Today we can break down Twain's comment into a handful of issues: the definition of "the wild," the human desire to gaze at exotic species, and the conservation strategies that play out definitions of the wild and of the spectacular. In the late 1890s, when Twain made his observation, the term "game" generally referred to the objects of recreational sport, as it does today. Now the wild has become a consumer item, "game" for our jaded sensibilities, whether we are out to kill it or to observe it. So too are "natives"—Indigenous peoples living traditional lives. Happily, the propensity for European settlers to regard Indigenous peoples as shooting targets has largely ceased. Instead, they have become spectacle. In New Zealand, for instance, tourists can take one-day bus tours to Rotorua, where they can "experience Māori customs and traditions" by wandering through a village established precisely to satisfy their desire to see, smell, and taste a fabricated version of Indigenous life.[7]

Twain also included "lecturers" in his list of "game" missing from the landscape. Twain was a lecturer—he was in Australia because he expected to be paid for entertaining the locals. He was accustomed to being subject to his audience's gaze; his insight was that wild animals and natives had also been turned into performers for spectators' gratification. The process has continued into our time, evolving into our dominant means for preserving what we have left of the wild. Removed and controlled—into cages, reserves, reservations, stages, and screens—animals, Indigenous peoples, and entertainers satisfy our desire for the exotic while keeping us safely on the other side of the glass.

7
Chameleons

PART I: RACE, GENDER, TWAIN

My uncle Leonard cross-dressed. It was his idea of a party stunt. He'd come out of the bedroom carrying my aunt's purse over his wrist and wearing her hat, gloves, heels, jewelry, hose, garter belt, and slip. Maybe a smear of lipstick. Rarely a dress. He'd mince around the house imitating her. I sensed aggression but didn't know how to name it, so I laughed along with the grown-ups because I didn't know what else to do. They probably didn't know what else to do, either. I doubt they knew any more about transvestism than I did.

There's a picture of Mark Twain in women's clothes, too. He had taken part in one of the family's theatricals, choosing a female role. In the photo he's wearing a dress and bonnet and kicking up his feet. He looks really happy.

A lot of men cross-dress in Twain's fiction. As do a number of women. Until recently, almost nobody paid attention to these episodes. Before I read Linda Morris's 2007 *Gender Play in Mark Twain: Cross-Dressing and Transgression*, I dismissed stories like "How Nancy Jackson Married Kate Wilson" and various cross-dressing episodes in works like *Huck Finn* and "Wapping Alice" as a form of low-order farce. I've never liked farce, though these days I've learned to appreciate some of its great artists. Linda Morris was part of my education; she taught me to look beyond the sheer buffoonery of Twain's cross-dressing characters and try to understand where he's going with them. Since then I've been thinking about Twain's cross-dressing characters alongside his mixed-race characters. Bringing them together has helped me understand just how interested he was in "inbetweenness," the "both/and" rather than the "either/or," and how culture—ours and those of other countries—dictates how we perceive individuals who live in the interstices between locally dictated categories.

Those interstices, the state of "inbetween," is also one of those arenas where Twain's and my interests converge across our temporal divide. Intellectually, I'm fascinated by the imaginative spaces that "both/and"

Figure 8. Twain and daughter Susy as Hero and Leander, family theatrical, 1890; courtesy of the Mark Twain Project, Bancroft Library, University of California, Berkeley.

opens up, in terms of both gender and race. I'm interested in how we perceive cross-race and cross-gender people and in how crossing over can both free and constrict individual lives. My interests are personal, too, and not just because of Uncle Len: as a black/white couple with a mixed-race daughter, racial "inbetweenness" has been part of Billy's, my, and our daughter Kate's family dynamic, from comparing skin colors at the dinner table to the dilemma of choosing racial identity on college application forms. At the same time, rearing a child during the decades when it became possible to talk about homosexuality radically increased my awareness of the emerging visibility of multiple gender identities and some of their similarities to cross-race identities. In talking to Kate about friends with same-sex parents, or friends struggling to define their own sexuality, I began to map a new territory, one that tracks changes in social perceptions of both mixed-race and cross-gender people.

My travels in Twain's wake broadened my interest, alerting me to the many ways that race and gender plot across cultures. In New Delhi in 2013 we attended a protest staged in response to the resurrection of repressive antisodomy laws first promulgated in the 1860s. The speakers included a group of Hijra, individuals born biologically male but who live as female and speak of themselves as "neither man nor woman but both man and woman." I was struck by their self-confidence, their sense of a secure identity. The protest was effective, too: since 2014 Hijra, along with other transgender people, have been legally recognized as a third sex by the Indian government—a significant marker in the country's move toward its recent definitive repeal of that 1861 "Section 377" antisodomy law. Closer to home, Canada just passed a law permitting third sex designation on Canadian passports. Though the United States has (in fits, starts, and backtracks) now recognized gay marriage, here transgender individuals still battle for recognition. In light of the history of mixed-race people in the United States, that's not surprising. Our culture resists the idea that "inbetweenness" can be an identity unto itself. We tend to be fixated on what inbetween individuals are *not*, rather than on what they are. Amazingly, given his era and social environment, Mark Twain was onto this—not as someone looking to establish independent third sex or mixed-race categories, but as part of his constitutional probing into the difference between appearance and reality. He was, in his own way, an epistemologist, an inquirer into the foundations of knowledge, of how we can verify what we think we know. Given the time in which he lived, race and gender crossings provided him with ample material for his quest.

All Mark Twain scholars know a lot about Mark Twain and race—the topic has come with the territory for the last fifty years or more—but Mark Twain and gender is a relatively new area, which is why I used to dismiss Twain's cross-dressing characters as farce. There has to be a vocabulary and conceptual framework for us to recognize what we are seeing, and my training didn't provide me with any way of seeing and articulating cross-gender issues. I finally became interested in Twain's gender bending in the mid-1990s, around the time I was helping Kate navigate the shoals of race and gender in junior high. I was writing about Twain's unpublished short story "1002nd Arabian Night." In the tale's fictive Middle Eastern culture, the visible marker of gender identity is the side of the head that one's hair is parted on. In the story a witch switches the part in the hair of two babies of the opposite sex, with the result that the girl is perceived as a boy and the boy as a girl. The parents are so blinded by gender conventions that they can't tell the biological male from the biological female even when the kids are naked in the bath. The boy is raised as a girl and the girl as a boy; the high point of the story comes after the two have grown up, married, and reproduced, culminating in the appearance of the putative male giving birth and the putative female's announcement that "the miracle of miracles has come to pass . . . not I but my husband is the child's mother!" Throughout this story Twain gleefully plays with gender pronouns—the putative male is referred to as "she" instead of "he" and the putative female as "he" instead of "she"—and with the social response to their behaviors—the dreamy, romantic "he" is considered a "milksop" and the active, aggressive "she" is "defective."

This is a story about gender's social construction, about the cultural cues that enable us to read it. I don't think Twain intended "1002nd Arabian Night" to be about transgendering (not that he knew the term), but the story's burlesque—or maybe it's carnavalesque—foregrounding of cross-dressing and cross-gender behavioral cues, culminating in the "father" giving physical birth to the baby, comes mighty close. In other stories, such as "Hellfire Hotchkiss," about a girl who prefers boys' activities, he focuses on the behavioral conventions dictating (or not) gender. Although he had no word to describe it, it's clear that Twain perceived that sexual organs and gender behaviors were not inextricably linked. If we plot his gender-experimental characters on a gender-behavior continuum, I think we would discover that Twain identified a wide variety of gender "positions" in the human spectrum. Which doesn't mean that he exactly understood what to do with them, or that he had a vocabulary to describe them or even that he was particularly comfortable with them. What he did understand was that appearance was not reality, that appearance—what we see or think we see—is funneled through cultural beliefs that are manifested in the materialities of custom, like clothing, hairstyles, or approved behaviors. Reality was that murky underside, where little was as it seemed and unnamable truths lurked in an indefinite arena of the inbetween.

So he became a literary comedian. Like many trans comedians today, Twain cast most of his gender-crossing incidents as farce because comedy defused his readers' tensions and nudged them to imagine other forms of gender identity. "Humor is the great thing, the saving thing after all. The minute it crops up, all our hardnesses yield, all our irritations and resentments flit away, and a sunny spirit takes their place," Twain commented in a late essay ("What Paul Bourget Thinks of Us," 1895). At a session on "Performing Gender" I attended at the 2017 Brooklyn Book Festival, Olivier Py, writer, director, and cross-dressing actor, commented that cross-gender performances affect onlookers as if "identity were a dream," and their response is to laugh. Writer and actor Peggy Shaw, also on the panel, said that cross-dressing performances make gender fluidity visible. "We are trying to change the power dynamic in the world so that we can be ourselves," she noted. "My shows are for making things that weren't there before." Both actors agreed that the introduction of gender "fluidity," as a concept and as a word, is both new and liberating. Twain's gender-crossing comedies work similarly, I think. He grasped the concept even if he didn't have the vocabulary to describe it. He didn't play cross-gender as much as he played cross-raciality, but he played it.

Once I began to wrap my head around Twain's dives into gender indeterminacy, I realized that they dovetail with his interest in racial ambiguity, and that both are cast in terms of people "reading" race and gender through cultural cues like clothes, manners, or behavior. In tandem with the rest of his generation, Twain was born into an America that craved definitive criteria for establishing identities. I sometimes see nineteenth-century America as suffering an epistemological crisis caused by the mixing of races and immigrant ethnicities (not to speak of women demanding greater social and political power). The response was a public demand for precise definitions of what a given individual "actually" "was." Popular magazines featured articles with titles like "What Is a Man?" and "What Constitutes a Woman?" The most pressing question, however, concerned racial definitions.

Americans' obsession with race led to elaborate systems of color gradations and "scientifically" measured racial inheritance. By the time Sam Clemens came along, people (white people in particular) had been subdividing races (black people in particular) along color lines for years. And with reason; there were a lot of mixed-race people out there, mostly because white male slave owners raped the women they held in bondage. By the mid-nineteenth century the US population could be plotted along a wide chromatic spectrum. Color gradations were socially significant even in slavery times, and in the post–Civil War period the game of determining whether a dark-skinned individual was a Negro-who-was-passing or was just a white-person-who-happened-to-be-dark could have deadly consequences for the person under scrutiny. The emerging ideology of white purity cast mixed-race individuals as racial pariahs: to be mixed meant to have inherited the worst character traits of both races. White pundits debated whether racially mixed people were even capable of making moral choices. The African American community evolved a racial imaginary that both inverted and reflected white ideology. There mixed-race individuals had the advantage, with the lightest winning the highest social status because they looked most like white people. These "advantages" had their downsides. The darker community thought their lighter brothers put on airs, especially if they adopted mainstream (white) patterns of taste and behavior. Moreover, being at the top of the African American color heap didn't much help relationships with the white community, which made sure that people of color, no matter what their hue, knew their "place" lower down on the racial pyramid. The result, as Charles Chesnutt's novels especially show, was confusion, mixed loyalties, and emotional anguish.

The system also created a chameleon effect—a sort of "epistemological-uncertainty-meets-racial-power-structure" intersection. It was more advantageous to be a light-skinned African American than a dark one, but it was still better to be almost any other race. The differences between "race" and what we call "ethnicity" were fairly blurry in the nineteenth century; for instance, an Italian, if not exactly white, was seen as a European, whereas a Jew was often regarded as another race entirely. Nevertheless it was better to be any of them than to be black. And so, like mixed-race Australian Aborigines, many mixed-race Americans passed themselves off as darker Europeans or Middle Easterners. One result was that a great many people assumed to be Italian, Spanish, or Middle Eastern were actually descendants of African and European acts of "amalgamation"—the nineteenth-century term for interracial sex. The reverse was true as well—anyone with dark skin could be taken for black. One of my family's stories was about dark-skinned Uncle Julian, one of my dad's brothers and 100 percent Ashkenazi Jewish, who was refused entry to the segregated hospital in Washington, DC, where my brother was born, because the staff thought he was a light-skinned Negro. The family was divided over which aspect of this incident deserved outrage: that the hospital was segregated (Mom), or that Uncle Julian should be taken for black (Dad, Julian, and the rest of their family).

Julian's experience wouldn't have surprised Mark Twain. Samuel Clemens grew up in a slave state, and color discriminations of all kinds were part of his natal environment. There's no question that he was a racist when he started out; his letters especially show it, such as the one the eighteen-year-old Sam Clemens wrote his mother about the sights he saw on his first trip East. "When I saw the Court House in Syracuse," he confides, "it called to mind the time when it was surrounded with chains and companies of soldiers, to prevent the rescue of McReynolds' nigger, by the infernal abolitionists. I reckon I had better black my face, for in these Eastern States niggers are considerably better than white people."[1] As the editors of Twain's letters note, Clemens's association of the Syracuse Court House with the widely publicized 1851 rescue of a fugitive slave by local antislavery activists gives a good indication of his racial politics at the time. I also see it as the self-conscious remark of an eighteen-year-old proud of his talent for putting together snappy sentences.

The important point, though, is that Clemens changed. It wasn't a sudden conversion, but rather a long experiential process. This included getting to know white abolitionists—Livy's parents, for instance, whose Elmira church had split over slavery and who had demonstrated their values by hosting Frederick Douglass on his lecture tours through New York State. Travel also broadened Twain's horizons. By the time he published *Adventures of Huckleberry Finn* (1884) he had rethought slavery; by the time he published *The Tragedy of Pudd'nhead Wilson* (1893) he was deeply engaged in rethinking the concept of race altogether.

Pudd'nhead Wilson has become a (perhaps *the*) central text for scholars studying Twain's writings about race and gender, because it is all about race and gender crossings. The novella focuses on the fate of Roxy, a fair, mixed-race slave, and on the two little boys she cares for—one her even whiter son (Roxy is 1/16 black, her son is 1/32), and the other the "pure" white son of her master and his wife. In "1002nd Arabian Night" the gender-determining convention was the part in the hair: after the witch switches the babies' parts (it suddenly occurs to me [duh!] that Twain may have intended "part" as a pun here), no one can tell that the girl is really a boy and the boy a girl. In *Pudd'nhead Wilson* the race-determining factor is clothes—or rather, their absence. The baby boys in Roxy's care are unmistakably slave and master as long as the master's son is dressed in fine clothing and the slave's son is dressed in rough cottons, but they are indistinguishable when they are naked. So Roxy swaps their clothes, and as a consequence, their race and social place. The rest of the tale plays out the significance of her move.

It wasn't until I brought these two stories together that I realized that Twain really did understand that both race and gender are, as he says of race in *Pudd'nhead Wilson*, "fictions of law and custom." The fact that the children in both *Pudd'nhead Wilson* and "1002nd Arabian Night" need particular hairstyles or clothes to be race or gender identifiable points to Twain's insight that the cues we take as indications of gender or race are as much a product of our social environment as of genetic scripting. In both stories bath time is the significant setting: Roxy realizes the boys are interchangeable after her master, dropping in while she is bathing them, asks which one is his. In "1002nd Arabian Night" the parents see only the "parts" in the hair that they believe indicate gender, even when they are observing their naked offspring in the bath. We see—know—only through the dark glasses of our cultures' social codings.

I should note that I'm not the first person to mull the confluence of clothes and both racial and gender crossings in Mark Twain's work. The topic has fascinated scholars for at least the last twenty years—since race and especially gender became "visible" in scholarly discourse. Marjorie Garber noted it in *Vested Interests*, her 1992 study of cross-dressing, and Linda Morris treats it extensively in *Gender Play in Mark Twain*, where she examines the multiple incidents of cross-dressing in *Pudd'nhead Wilson*, especially by characters like Roxy who are also cross-race. In one telling incident in the story, Morris reminds us, Roxy (who to all outward appearances is white) disguises herself as a black male. At that point, Morris comments, Roxy becomes "'every man' and 'every woman'; she is black *and* white, male *and* female" (80). Later Roxy's son Tom mirrors her act by blackening his features and assuming women's clothes. Morris concludes that "*Pudd'nhead Wilson* ultimately insists that race and gender are interconnected performances that are multicultural and highly unstable" (87).

Pretty much all the writers on gender and race in *Pudd'nhead Wilson* envision the story solely within US cultural contexts. But if this project has taught me anything, it's that systems of power like race and gender (and by "systems of power" I mean cultural codes that define and therefore control individual identities) are rarely confined to national boundaries, at least not in our highly interconnected world. Morris's recognition that Roxy is "both male *and* female" kicks us into international third sex territory, and her reminder that Roxy is "black *and* white" takes us to areas of the world, like South Africa, that (unlike the United States) recognize cross-race people as categories unto themselves. Roxy's and Tom's "performance" of gender and race looks different if we think of them within global contexts, and that's what I want to do here—not with the text of *Pudd'nhead Wilson*, but with the themes of race and gender crossings that *Pudd'nhead Wilson* opens up and that thread through *Following the Equator*. One of my project's objectives was first to explore how Twain's perception of the social construction of race and gender percolate through *Following*, and then to see whether I could perceive any legacies of what he saw as I traveled in his wake. Not surprisingly, South Africa turned out to be the country where questions about identity and visibility surged to the forefront, not because of what Twain wrote about it, but because of what he *didn't* write. Moreover, as a white Jewish woman and a light-skinned black man traveling through twenty-first-century South Africa, Billy and I seemed to epitomize the enigma of identity ourselves.

PART II: APPEARANCE AND REALITY IN SOUTH AFRICA, 1896: THE JAMESON RAID

Most readers, myself included, find the South Africa portion of *Following the Equator* the least satisfactory section of the book. It is short compared to the India and Australasia sections, and the topics it covers, while clearly of interest historically, don't let us into Twain's thoughts very often. He told his friend and financial adviser Henry Huttleston Rogers that one reason he was happy to cut the book back from a projected two volumes to one was that in order to create a two-volume set "it would be necessary to make South Africa take up a great deal of room, in order to fill out—a country which was absolutely barren of interest when I was there, except the *political* interest—a matter which is as dead as Adam today, & will never be resurrected by me, during this life" (*Mark Twain's Correspondence with Henry Huttleston Rogers* 274; italics in original). Hence the brevity of the section. The only aspects of the country that receive more than a few paragraphs are the Trappist monastery outside Durban (giving Twain opportunity to rant about the perversity of human nature), the technicalities of diamond mining (new to Twain), and what his letter to Rogers refers to as "the *political* interest"—otherwise known as the Jameson Raid. I'm going to focus on the raid because the amount of effort Twain expended trying to understand what it was all about suggests that he saw it as an appearance/reality puzzle, and that as such, the raid modeled the difficulties of "knowing" in a country where appearance and reality resided in a seemingly permanent disconnect.

A little background. In 1896 South Africa was divided between the British, who controlled what was then known as the Cape Colony, and the Dutch-descended Boers, who controlled the Orange Free State and the Transvaal, including the new cities of Pretoria and Johannesburg. However, many English speakers, including Americans, lived in Johannesburg, the majority of them engineers working in the diamond and gold mines nearby. The Jameson Raid was orchestrated by the entrepreneur, imperialist, and Cape Colony prime minister Cecil Rhodes, and it was carried out by Rhodes's close friend Leander Starr Jameson. Rhodes's game plan was to encourage English-speaking residents of Boer-controlled Johannesburg to revolt against the Boer government, for the whole thing to get big and nasty enough for the British to step in, and for the Empire to finally take the Transvaal under British control—a move that would greatly benefit Rhodes himself, since he was the major owner of the mines in Boer country. In retrospect we can see the Jameson Raid as a prelude to the Anglo-Boer War (1899–1902); writing in 1896–1897, Twain saw it as a postscript to the Boer War of 1880–1881. Twain, who liked to play the military strategist even while candidly admitting his utter lack of military experience, satirizes the Jameson Raid when he writes it up for *Following the Equator*. As we saw in his mock itinerary for Hindu pilgrims, Twain had a habit of satirizing phenomena he couldn't understand. In South Africa he satirized the Jameson Raid because he couldn't figure out what the raiders thought they could accomplish.

At the time of the raid, Rhodes's scheme was invisible. The raid was pitched as a defense of the English-speaking minority in Johannesburg, who had been seeking representation in the Boer government. Heavily taxed, but without representation or legal permission to establish their own institutions (such as schools), the English speakers called themselves "Reformers" and were trying to work out a deal with the local authorities. However, some were also smuggling guns into the English enclave, an act that made the Boer government highly suspicious of their intentions. The raid was supposed to come to those men's defense, and in so doing to spark an armed uprising. It flopped, mostly because it was poorly organized, badly run, and effectively leaked. When Jameson and his men crossed into Boer territory the Boers were ready for them, and the raiders—those who weren't picked off by Boer marksmen—were captured and imprisoned. A number of Johannesburg Reformers were also arrested and jailed as accomplices.

The whole thing intrigued Twain, and he devotes two unusually long chapters to detailing the raid. He did a lot of research before he wrote the chapters, in an earnest effort to understand what was really going on. He had arrived in South Africa four months after the raid, and while he was there he discussed South African politics with the locals as often as possible, including interviewing Reformers who were being held in Pretoria's prison. Adèle Le Bourgeois Chapin, an American from Louisiana living in Johannesburg, left a record of Twain's association with the Reformers while he was in the Transvaal in her memoir, *"Their Trackless Way": A Book of Memories*, published by her daughter in 1931. The memoir includes an account of Adèle Le Bourgeois Chapin's time in South Africa, where her husband, Robert Williams Chapin, had partnered with John C. Manion to supply equipment from the Ingersoll-Sergeant Rock and Drill Company (later to become Ingersoll Rand) to Cecil Rhodes's mines in the Transvaal. Robert Chapin, who had for a time owned Ingersoll-Sergeant Rock and Drill, provided the conduit to South Africa. His partner, Manion, who had preceded him to South Africa, also served as US consul in Johannesburg, having been appointed by President Grover Cleveland. According to Adèle Chapin, Manion left when her husband arrived, and Robert Chapin took over the position as consul. His exact title isn't clear; Natalie Hammond refers to him as the US consul at Johannesburg in her memoir *A Woman's Part in a Revolution* (1897), but the *Papers Relating to the Foreign Relations of the United States* lists Chapin as acting consular agent (405), which is also the title under which he signed himself when he turned in a report on commodity prices in the South African republic (i.e., Boer country) on September 18, 1896. Whether he served as consul or acting consul, it's clear that Robert Chapin was involved in British/ Boer South Africa on both the economic and political fronts. As Adèle Chapin puts it: "From that moment [when the partner left], we were in the thick of it" (114).

Enter Mark Twain. Twain appears in Adèle Chapin's memoir three times, twice in Boer South Africa. The first appearance is in Pretoria, where Twain attended a dinner party with the Chapins, Mrs. John Jay Hammond, and James Rose Innes, a South African lawyer who would go on to serve as the country's chief justice from 1914 to 1927. Absent was John Hammond, one of the Reformers who had been arrested as accomplices to the raiders. Hammond was still being held, but his death sentence had just been commuted, and although no one yet knew exactly what his new sentence would be, the dinner celebrated the commutation. The Hammonds, too, were Americans, acquaintances of Twain's from years before. One of the many American mining engineers recruited to work in the goldfields of the Transvaal (also Boer territory), Hammond had been overseeing Rhodes's South African mines, a position he would quit after the debacle of the raid. Adèle considered him "one of the great-est mining engineers on the Rand" (114). James Rose Innes was South African born and bred. Adèle Chapin thought him a wise man, someone who "belongs to the judicial type who holds all life in balance in his mind and sees it steadily and sees it whole" (122).

If Twain had not been introduced to South African politics before this, the Pretoria dinner must have done so. For starters, the participants all had some professional relationship to Cecil Rhodes. Robert Chapin and John Hammond supplied expertise and equipment to Rhodes's mines. Rose Innes *had* worked for Rhodes; he had served as Rhodes's attorney general of the Cape Colony from 1890 to 1893, but he had quit in protest over Rhodes's economic and racial policies. By the time of the dinner he had become Rhodes's critic. Rigorously honest and sensitive to the white settlers' marginalization of the Indigenous black population, Innes was appalled by Rhodes's administration. Rhodes, he claimed, had "infected public life with a virus."[2]

Twain must have made a good impression on the Chapins, because on May 29 they invited him to a major political event at their house in

Johannesburg. (Pretoria and Johannesburg are about thirty-five miles apart.) The first part of the evening featured a dinner to which, Adèle Chapin remembers, twenty of "the best and most conservative elements in Johannesburg" were invited. The second part featured another twenty "leading Boers" who had been invited for a postprandial gathering in the hopes, she claimed, "that if they could meet and talk things out it would lessen the bitterness of feeling." In *A Woman's Part in a Revolution* Natalie Hammond mentions that Robert Chapin was held in high esteem by both the foreign community and the Boers, so the Chapin home was a good location for outreach to the Boer community. In *Following the Equator* Twain claims that he "had no personal access to Boers—their side was a secret to me, aside from what I was able to gather of it from published sources" (657), but his presence at the party in Johannesburg suggests otherwise. On that evening Twain was present while both sides hotly discussed their conflicts, and he seems to have felt confident enough in his grasp of the issues to intervene. Chapin's account focuses on herself (after all, it's her memoir), but it gives us a fair picture of Twain's involvement.

At the close of dinner—before the English speakers retired to the drawing rooms to meet with the Boers—Adèle Chapin (who was hosting alone, her husband having been unexpectedly called to Pretoria) proposed a toast "to the United States and to South Africa—England's oldest and youngest children" and invited Twain to address the topic. His talk, which Chapin reports as "going deep into the recesses of history, touching upon the psychology of nationality," claimed that Americans had revolted not against England but against England's then-current policies, policies that the mother country later disavowed. In other words, Twain targeted the evils of party loyalty rather than British identity. In Australia Twain had been criticized for taking sides in a local political dispute. Clearly, by the time he reached South Africa he had learned how to navigate the shoals between the British Empire and its increasingly restless colonials. Here he seems to sympathize with the Reformers—who were being castigated back in London—while at the same time taking care not to impugn England itself.

Fired by this and other toasts, the company left the dinner table to meet the Boers. The cultural divide was visible, especially to the Americans. I think it's significant that they read it through clothes. "None of the Boers were in evening dress," Chapin recalls. "Most of them had long beards, and kind, earnest faces; they were all burghers. In the charged atmosphere of the room, talk soon became intense, and I remember a feeling sweeping over me that this was like a salon of the French Revolution." Her next memory also pivoted on clothes. Twain took Chapin aside and asked her to address the Boers. She had made a great impression on them, he told her, adding, "Why, they have never seen a woman before in evening dress." Victorian fashion of the time featured bared necks and shoulders and often arms; Twain seemed to think that the spectacle of a self-possessed, articulate woman in formal (and in Boer eyes, daring) dress would captivate the provincial burghers. "Anything you say would have great influence," he told her. "I want you to speak to them." Chapin, a southern lady, first demurred but then allowed herself to be persuaded. Twain rapped on the piano to get the crowd's attention and then introduced her. "I spoke," she records, "for twenty minutes. When I finished speaking some of the Boers were kissing my hands and saying 'wass muss man faagt? (What must we do?).' I have no idea what I said," Chapin recalls. "I would not believe I had spoken at all, if I had not a letter from Mark Twain, written the following day, 30th May 1896. In it he said: 'Do you know you should have been an advocate—you got at the deep places in our hearts, Friday night. It was a strong, moving speech. It made me want to follow and endorse and applaud'" (Chapin 122–24).

This lengthy quotation from Chapin's memoir hands us a lot of information. First, it gives the lie to Twain's assertion that he never met Boers. Second, it shows how engaged Mark Twain was by the South African political scene and implies that the British and Americans living in Boer country trusted Twain enough to invite him to their highly charged political events. That he felt that he could ask his hostess to make a speech in a political situation to which he was a stranger also suggests that he felt he had been taken into the community and made a part of it. Twain's May 30 note to Adèle also corroborates her account of the evening. He boarded an 11:00 P.M. train for Bloemfontein right after the event, and he must have written his note to Adèle on the journey (Philippon 18). Finally, and not incidentally, Adèle's account also reminds us of the cultural weight costume bore in defining identity and social status for both Americans. "I had on a lovely gown," she remembered later, "and to it I attribute my influence with the Boers" (122). Twain seems to have agreed.

Twain continued his research into the South Africa situation when he returned to London. During the fall of 1896 and winter of 1897 he consumed the newspapers, books, and journal articles that were volubly responding to the raid and its aftermath, including, he tells us, *South Africa as It Is* (1897), by F. Reginald Statham ("an able writer partial to the Boers"); *The Story of an African Crisis, Being the Truth about the Jameson*

*Raid and Johannesburg Revolt of 1896, Told with the Assistance of the Lead-
ing Actors of the Drama* (1897), by Edmund Garrett and E. J. Edwards ("a
brilliant writer partial to Rhodes"); and *A Woman's Part in a Revolution*
(1897), by Natalie Harris (Mrs. John Hays) Hammond ("a vigorous and
vivid diarist, partial to the Reformers") (*FE* 660). We know from Chapin's
memoir that Twain dined (again) with the Hammonds in Pretoria just
after John Hays Hammond's release from prison. Twain clearly did his
due diligence in reading around all sides of the story, but between Rose
Innes and the Hammonds in Pretoria, and the Johannesburg evening's
earnest attempt to encourage dialogue on a face-to-face basis, Twain's
sympathies seem to have been co-opted by the Reformers' original narrative about struggling for visibility within the Boer power structure. By
the time Twain left South Africa, most of the Reformers themselves realized that they had been tools of Rhodes's attempt to so inflame English/
Boer relations that the British government would intervene and (in
Rhodes's best-case scenario) annex the Transvaal. "All the reformers I
met agreed that the cause of political reform has been retarded a decade
by the Jameson fiasco," Twain told the *Chicago Daily Tribune* when he
reached England that summer.[3] The apparent hadn't proved real. The
deeper Twain delved, the murkier the whole incident became.

Which brings Cecil Rhodes—the "reality"—from behind the scenes.
Twain didn't like Rhodes, and he aims some of his most lethal bullets at him. This initially puzzled me, because I would have expected
Twain to admire Rhodes. In 1897 Twain had not yet evolved into the
anti-imperialist he was to become—indeed, he has ample praise for the
British in India, and we see his careful dancing around British colonial
policies in his toast at the Chapins' home. Meeting the Boer burghers
there doesn't seem to have given him much respect for the ordinary Boer,
either; although he evinced some regard for the Boer government, he
certainly didn't see the Boer population as helpless victims of Rhodes's
imperialist greed, as he had described the Aborigines whose lands the
settlers had seized in Australia. He also admired great entrepreneurs,
and Rhodes was certainly a great entrepreneur. Just because Rhodes
used well-meaning if gullible people to engineer a power grab wouldn't
automatically villainize him in Twain's eyes.

But Rhodes's reputation was slippery—indeterminate—and I think
Twain disliked him in part because he couldn't get a fix on who or what
South Africa's most towering figure actually was. Twain comes back to
him in the penultimate chapter of the book. After discoursing on gold
and diamond mining, on the Boer character (pious, racist, and ignorant),

and on the "tamed and Christianized blacks" (who reminded Twain of
the African American slaves of his childhood), Twain returns to Rhodes.
"Before the middle of July," Twain records, "we reached Cape Town, and
the end of our African journeyings. And well satisfied; for, towering above
us was Table Mountain—a reminder that we had now seen each and all of
the great features of South Africa except Mr. Cecil Rhodes" (FE 708).

Rhodes, the never seen, then replaces Table Mountain as the central feature of South Africa. Twain does not describe the man himself.
Instead he focuses on Rhodes's reflection in other peoples' eyes. The fact
that public opinion about Rhodes was so equally divided rankled him.
"Whether Mr. Rhodes is the lofty and worshipful patriot and statesman
that multitudes believe him to be, or Satan come again, as the rest of
the world account him, he is still the most imposing figure in the British empire outside of England," he begins. Rhodes's fame, the attention
his every act receives, and the awe he inspires are unprecedented, Twain
claims. Significantly, few are willing to criticize him openly. "It was as if
he were deputy-God on the one side, deputy-Satan on the other, proprietor
of the people, able to make them or ruin them by his breath, worshiped
by many, hated by many, but blasphemed by none among the judicious,
and even by the indiscreet in guarded whispers only" (FE 708–9). The
rest of the chapter is given to the binary nature of Rhodes's reputation,
the continuing arguments over the sources of his success and the continuation of his dominance. "One fact is sure," Twain comments, "he keeps
his prominence and a vast following, no matter what he does," including
persuading his followers to support him even as he moves against their
own interests. Twain concludes, "He has done everything he could think
of to pull himself down to the ground; he has done more than enough to
pull sixteen common-run great men down; yet there he stands, to this
day, upon his dizzy summit under the dome of the sky, an apparent per-
manency, the marvel of the time, the mystery of the age, an Archangel
with wings to half the world, Satan with a tail to the other half" (FE 710).

The binary nature of this description is deliberate; there are no gray
areas in this portrait. What Twain doesn't mention is that Rhodes may
have been gay. Never married, apparently uneasy even in the presence
of women, Cecil Rhodes lived in an intensely homosocial environment.
He employed no women in his Cape Town mansion and avoided social
contacts with women when he could. He lived with one young man, Nev-
ille Pickering, for five years, until Pickering's death in 1886, after which
he chose Jameson as his domestic partner. Though neither "homosex-
ual" nor "domestic partner" was a common term in 1896, discussions of

sexual variations had been ongoing in the West since at least the Greeks, and both religious and civic laws regulating sexual intercourse (not only with whom, but how) had existed since the early Christian era. By the 1860s the British colonial government had begun instituting antisodomy laws across the Empire, perhaps to cover up the fact that the men who ruled Britannia's waves had created an overwhelmingly homosocial environment for themselves. "The British Empire was trying not to have women," South African scholar Isabel Hofmeyr told me drily, when I asked her about Rhodes's sexuality. Despite often being married to women, the men of the colonial establishment circulated through a male world, where they formed what Hofmeyr described as a "continuum of attachments" that were both social and erotic.

All of which leaves determining sexual behavior in the past extremely difficult. Maybe Rhodes was gay and maybe he wasn't. A number of books and articles argue one side or another, but nothing seems to be proven. Even so, Rhodes's lifestyle had to be the topic of some of those "guarded whispers" to which Twain refers. Indeed, in my research I came across a 1902 article from New Zealand, titled "Cecil Rhodes as a Woman Hater," which mentions the dearth of female servants and the "many stories current about the great South African statesman's misogyny."⁴ If the gossip had reached as far as New Zealand in 1902, I'm sure Twain heard it in Cape Town in 1896. Rhodes's sexuality remains of popular interest, by the way; the information tape on the Hop On Hop Off bus Billy and I took around Cape Town chatted to us about Rhodes's young men, and the women he rebuffed. Contemporary South Africa's gay-friendly policies don't seem to have mitigated the thrill of speculating about Rhodes's sexual proclivities, which testifies to his lingering domination of the South African imagination.

The point is that you can't trust what you see—or think you see. Twain paints Rhodes in either/or terms because there was no consensus about who he was—angel or demon, destroyer or savior. His focus is all on Rhodes's reputation, on how other people read him. Which takes us back to Roxy and Tom and their multiple disguises, and to the vexed question of identity and visibility they represent. It also highlights Twain's comments on clothes, which occur, randomly but tellingly, throughout the South Africa section. The reason Twain notices the "tamed and Christianized" blacks is that they wore Western clothes, which Twain describes as "fiendish." "But for that, many of them would have been remarkably handsome," he opines. "Often where all the other aspects were strikingly and harmoniously and thrillingly African, a flock

of these natives would intrude, looking wholly out of place, and spoil it
all, making the thing a grating discord, half African and half American" (*FE* 692–93). Note: it's not the clothes themselves that Twain objects
to (though he does deem Western clothes "dowdy"); it's the garments'
ability to make bodies seem what they are not, half one thing and half
another. He had recorded a similar rant about Western dress on native
schoolchildren in Ceylon, but there he focused more on the ugliness of
the clothes themselves, especially in contrast to the "Oriental conflagra-
tions of [native] costume!" that otherwise made Indian streets pulse with
color. Here it's the fact that Africans are wearing Western clothes that
disconcerts him. For Twain, Western dress on African bodies is illegible,
unreadable, evoking a kind of being that he does not know how to identify or name. "Later," he tells us, he followed a group of "Colored" women
around King William's Town, imagining them to be the slave women of
his childhood. This is the only time Twain uses the term "Colored" in
the entire South Africa section, and it's hard to know whether he was
actually distinguishing between black and "Colored," as South Africans
did, or merely referring to Negroes as "Colored," as Americans did. In
any case, they first attracted, then baffled him. "I seemed among old, old
friends; friends of fifty years, and I stopped and cordially greeted them,"
he reports. When they answered in their native tongue he was star-
tled: "I did not understand a word they said. I was astonished; I was not
dreaming that they would answer in anything but American" (*FE* 693).
The clothes (and, he notes, the timbre of the women's voices) deceived
Twain, drifting him back to the securities of childhood, when he knew
(or thought he knew) who and what people were. It fascinates me that
Twain used this anecdote as an escape to his personal, American past,
rather than as a window onto South Africa's present. King William's
Town had a prominent black elite (as Cape Town had a prominent "Colored" elite) at the turn of the twentieth century, and these women could
well have been members of South Africa's emerging black and "colored"
upper and middle classes. Instead of exploring the sociology of race that
the women's clothes suggested, Twain makes them illegible to American
eyes. The women of King William's Town presented him with a text he
professed not to know how to read.

Not so the Boers. In the same chapter in which Twain describes
the African women, he describes Boer dress. No ambiguity here: class,
clothes, and ethnicity all come together. The group he targets are the
farmers, the "Boers of the veldt." In India Twain had watched the crowds
in railway stations and rhapsodized over the harmony of Indian clothing,

the variety of colors that all seemed perfectly blended. He observes the Boers in a railway station too, but comes to the opposite evaluation. "At a village station," he remembers, "a hundred of them got out of the third-class cars to feed." The word "feed" instantly signals that the Boers are barely human, and Twain continues the attack. The men he sees in the station are country "louts," with "hideous" clothes to match their characters. Unlike the masses in Indian railroad stations, the Boers' clothes are "miracles of ugly colors unharmoniously associated" (FE 694). They live like animals, too. "The Boer gets up early and sets his 'niggers' to their tasks . . . ; eats, smokes, drowses, sleeps; toward evening superintends the milking, etc; eats, smokes, drowses; goes to bed at early candlelight in the fragrant clothes he (and she) have worn all day and every week-day for years" (697). Twain claims to have heard this description of Boer life from another passenger with whom he had chatted on the train, but he repeats it as if it were an official document. At least Twain had found one thing that was unambiguous in South Africa. He must have felt relieved.

Which brings us to the very last chapter of Following the Equator. Twain starts off with a brief list of what he saw in Cape Town. There's little embellishment to the list, other than his note that he listened while the members of Parliament "quarreled in two languages . . . and agreed in none" (FE 710). Then, for no apparent reason, he segues into an anecdote about Dr. James Barry, a woman who lived as a man and got away with it.

Twain encountered Dr. Barry's story via a painting in a private home, "a picture of a pale, intellectual young man in a pink coat with a high black collar" (FE 711). Barry, Twain learned, had come out from England with his regiment fifty years previously and, despite multiple incidents of misbehavior, including dueling, was never disciplined by the military headquarters. He was a favorite among the young women but never formed a relationship with any of them. He did excel as a doctor, including, Twain mentions, as an obstetrician. He died twenty years into his sojourn at the Cape, and it was then that it was discovered he was female.

The backstory, Twain learns, was that Barry "was a daughter of a great English house" who had come out to the Cape after disgracing herself at home. That's why she was never disciplined; the authorities back in England knew who she was. But no one in South Africa did. "She chose to change her name and her sex and take a new start in the world," Twain concludes.

Well. That's it, for Twain. He doesn't pursue the story or even comment on it, and Following the Equator ends two paragraphs later. Where does the story take us? Just before he reveals Barry's sex, Twain comments on his own writing: "The story seems to be arriving nowhere. But that is because I have not finished." A student of mine once pointed out that those two lines could describe Twain's entire book: a jumble of unconcluded and inconclusive anecdotes, stories drawn from all segments of his life and the globe, and brief but astute observations about the cultural convulsions the British Empire had fostered. But I wonder about the juxtapositioning of Twain's analysis of Rhodes and the story of Dr. Barry, along with his seemingly random comment about the legislators quarreling in two languages and agreeing in none, his investigation into the facts and fictions surrounding the raid, and his fragmentary notes about black Africans under British and Boer domination. And I wonder about the South African populations he did not mention, such as the large Indian community in Durban (he notes that he stayed in an "Indian hotel" in Durban, but not that there was a substantial Indian community there), or the even larger "Colored" community—the neither black nor Asian nor white residents of South Africa who, invisible in Twain's book, were nevertheless a recognized community even then. I also wonder whether the focus on Rhodes's legibility—on how he was read by different groups of people—and on Dr. Barry's transvestism aren't in some way Twain's attempt to point to the conundrum of identity in South Africa at the end of the nineteenth century. Barry's disguise, after all, was a matter of clothes. We've been there before. In South Africa nothing, it seemed, was what it appeared. Maybe one reason the South Africa section of *Following the Equator* is so short is that Twain realized just how challenging it would be to explore the gaps between appearance and reality there. It would take writing a whole other volume, and he certainly did not want to do that. So instead of delving, he skimmed, recording anecdotes and short narratives that pointed toward the country's identity complexities without ever naming them.

PART III: CHAMELEONS

In the Apartheid Museum in Johannesburg hangs a reproduction of a newspaper article from 1986. The article lists the number of people whose race had been changed the previous year. Titled "1985 Had at Least 1000 'Chameleons,'" the article reports that "more than 1000 people officially changed colour last year. They were reclassified from one race group to another by the stroke of a Government pen. Detail of what is dubbed 'the chameleon dance' were given in reply to Opposition questions in

Parliament. The Minister of Home Affairs, Mr. Stoffel Botha, disclosed that during 1985:

702 Coloured people became white.
19 whites became Coloured.
One Indian became white.
Three Chinese became white.
50 Indians became Coloured.
43 Coloureds became Indians.
21 Indians became Malay.
30 Malays went Indian.
249 blacks became Coloured.
20 Coloureds became black.
Two blacks became "other Asians."
One black was classified Griqua.
11 Coloureds became Chinese.
Three Coloureds went Malay.
One Chinese became Coloured.
Eight Malays became Coloured.
Three blacks were classed as Malay.
No blacks became white and no whites became black.

The Star, March 21, 1986

Did I neglect to mention that Twain begins his account of his South Africa sojourn with a description of a chameleon that lived in the courtyard of his Durban hotel? He characterizes it as "fat and indolent and contemplative," with a "froggy head" and "a back like a new grave" (*FE* 645). He was especially taken by the reptile's monocular vision, the fact that its eyes pivoted independently of each other. After his report on the chameleon he abruptly switches to notes about local customs and demography: "Natives must not be out after the curfew bell without a pass. In Natal there are ten blacks to one white. Sturdy plump creatures are the women" (645). Twain's description of the chameleon aside, the first two and a half pages of this section of *Following* read like jottings straight out of his notebooks—observations, with no probing as to cultural import or commentary about his own reactions.

When Billy and I visited South Africa in pursuit of Mark Twain, we were intrigued by the similarities and differences between that country's racial structure and our own. Parts of the history sound familiar;

even in 1896, when Twain visited, South Africa's shifting racial and ethnic composition in many ways mirrored that in the United States: to the large Indigenous African population, itself compounded of very different ethnic groups, was added a steady flow of immigrants, predominantly from Italy, the Russian Pale, and other southern and eastern European countries. South Africa had more British immigrants than the United States during that period, more Asians (the United States had put a stop to Chinese immigration fifteen years earlier), and a sizable influx of Indians (Mohandas Karamchand Gandhi, who would become the Mahatma, spent twenty-two years in South Africa during this time). At the top of both countries' racial heaps were the whites from Britain and northern Europe, who controlled pretty much everything worth controlling.

But South Africa acknowledged hybridity, whereas the United States did not. Rather than create multiple racial categories, as the French did in Louisiana and South Carolina, most American states classified mixed-race people according to their nonwhite component. As Roxy and her son's status demonstrated, in the United States having even one great-grandparent of color made one black—and in the pre–Civil War American South, also a slave. The result was that even after the war, most Americans could conceive of race only in either/or terms, and the words they used to describe an individual's race reflected their understanding of racial identity. Even when they recognized that racial mixing had occurred, mixed-race people were dismissed as "mulattoes" (if black/white) and "half-breeds" (if Indian/white)—rootless, placeless, and dangerous. Mixed-race individuals had no legal standing as such, which meant they had no collective identity or civil rights. In the late nineteenth century some African American intellectuals—W. E. B. Du Bois was one of them—pushed for the recognition of a mixed black/white "third race" in the United States, but the movement never gained traction.

In contrast, British South Africa distinguished racially mixed people from their "pure" progenitors, creating socially recognized racial groups and, in the process, encouraging a broader spectrum of racial definitions—a spectrum that laid the ground for apartheid's legal codification of racial groups in the 1940s. As I noted earlier, Twain never touches on the "Colored" (I put the word in scare quotes because it has a long and vexed history in South Africa) population in *Following*, and as far as I can tell he doesn't mention it in his notebooks or letters, either, which seems to me very curious. I would have thought that the author of *Pudd'nhead Wilson* would have been fascinated by South Africa's racial mixtures. As the *Star* article shows, South Africa's twentieth-century attempt to legally codify races and police their boundaries ended in absurdity; the very fact that the apartheid government could change an individual's race by fiat negates the premise that racial identities can be definitively determined.

I visited South Africa as a researcher, and race was definitely on my agenda, but the plunge into South Africa's racial designations turned out to be Billy's passion, not mine. Billy's parents were both light skinned but never tried to pretend they were white. Family albums going back four generations show various hues of middle-class African Americans. Clearly there had been white progenitors, but no one in the family knew who they were. Many family members have distinctly Native American characteristics, but although a few stories circulate about Blackfoot and Cherokee progenitors, the heritage isn't taken very seriously. So Billy never had any conflicts about identifying as a black American. But in South Africa, he suddenly wasn't black any more.

Because many of our Kansas University colleagues had professional connections in South Africa, we had access to some wonderful people across several racial communities there. Cape Town remains a major location for "Colored" communities, and we spoke with a number of "Colored" South Africans living in the area. Although South Africa has officially outlawed segregation, most people continue to live in areas whose racial boundaries were mandated under apartheid in the 1950s and 1960s, making for distinctly white, black, "Colored," or Indian communities. For me, having grown up in a Baltimore so segregated that its residents wouldn't have noticed if they woke up in apartheid South Africa, all this seemed familiar. I didn't like it, but I knew how to deal. And even if I didn't deal quite right, I was still—according to South Africa's classificatory system—white, and thus securely, if awkwardly, at the top of the hierarchy. For Billy, who grew up in a left-liberal village in Ohio, it was new, strange, and disquieting. Gone was the familiar sense of self as a black intellectual; instead he had to imagine himself as "Colored" and to feel his way through the very variegated "Colored" community. On the one hand, it was like finding a whole new batch of relatives. Our visits to private homes at times felt like visiting family: not only did folks look like him, but in one home we were both struck by a baby picture of the owner that looked exactly like a photo we have of Billy at the same age. The community's race pride and power assumptions were familiar, too, as was its condescension toward the darker, less successful black community. According to Mohamed Adhikari, who has explored racial identity in the South African "Colored" community, some South African "Coloreds" have always defined themselves by their racial and cultural ties to whiteness. Highly assimilationist, seeing themselves as very different from black South Africans, the "Colored" community, Adhikari argues, has historically used its white ancestry to demand social and political privileges, a positioning that implicitly—and for some, explicitly—makes them socially superior to the black community.

Although he comes from a light-skinned middle-class family, Billy has never identified with "aspiring" black Americans whose social institutions (like clubs and fraternities), dress, and manners imply social status superior to that of the larger black community. Not only has he "never identified"; he outright detests them. He brought that American framework to South Africa, and it contributed to his discomfort there. Suddenly he was being classed with the people he saw as, well, "dicty," trying to be white.

Mind you, no one throughout our entire month in South Africa ever referred to Billy in racial terms. This fascinated both of us. We had come unsure about our reception; were there interracial couples in South Africa? Would we be shunned? Attacked? We had married in the United States in 1968, exactly one year after the last "miscegenation" laws disappeared from the books. During the first twenty or so years of our marriage we were very careful where we went, rarely venturing into the South and ultracautious when our travels took us into the rural American West. The old fears and cautions came back as we checked into South African hotels and ventured into the streets. But Billy was a chameleon in South Africa. And as it turned out, so was I.

Being a chameleon isn't a new experience for my husband. He's even written poems about it. The southern Ohio area he comes from is home to many, many people of his hue, who identify themselves as black Americans and are seen as such by other races. When Billy began living in large coastal cities, however, people responded to him differently, often depending on neighborhood context. In New York especially, he can be greeted on the street by "hey bro," "hola amigo," or "salaam." He can also pass as just a gray-haired white guy. His skin color, hair, and facial features are ambiguous enough that he can fit more than one racial mold. I, on the other hand, am rarely seen as other than a white woman, and usually as a white Jewish woman. The Ashkenazi stamp came down hard on my features.

South Africa disturbed that sense of racial identity. This is how it worked out for us. We talked to many thoughtful and articulate people in South Africa, but we have mulled over two encounters in particular that seem to point out the illegibility of race in that country. The first was with a man I'll call Gerald near Cape Town, our first stop in South Africa.

We spent a long day with Gerald. "Cape Colored," he was born and reared in the area around Stellenbosch, a small city north of Cape Town where we spent our first weekend. He had grown up with one of our KU colleagues, and she arranged for us to meet him. The meeting turned into an eight-hour day, replete with a tour of the surrounding areas and lively discussion of South African racial attitudes.

Two things struck me about Gerald. The first was his sense of self, of confidence, sophistication, and power. He came by these both from family background and through his personal struggle to succeed against the odds. His is the story of an insider-outsider, a native who had to struggle to belong. He was born and reared in Stellenbosch, a pretty town boasting a rich, powerful university that, he informed us, was the ideological birthplace of apartheid. Stellenbosch reminded Billy and me of Santa Barbara, California. The two towns have the same air of wealth, the same proud preservation of a colonial past: Santa Barbara's architecture celebrates its founding by Spanish missionaries; Stellenbosch's celebrates its Dutch, "Boer" forebears. It's the kind of town where you can spend a pleasant day looking at old buildings and browsing through museums and shops. But we learned the city through Gerald's experience. A bright child, Gerald was college bound, but he couldn't go to Stellenbosch University, even though it was just down the road from his home. Stellenbosch was reserved for whites, so Gerald commuted to the University of the Western Cape, the only university in the area to which "Coloreds" were admitted. The University of the Western Cape is in a no-man's-land north of Cape Town, miles from Gerald's home. He remains bitter about the hours the commute took. After college he taught high school. He also became an activist, working against legal apartheid, and later on uplift projects in the black townships around Stellenbosch. He spent considerable time in England and the United States, in part to escape apartheid. Now retired, at the time we met him he was sitting on six boards. He remained engaged in uplift projects, including one to produce solar-powered lamps to replace candles in the settlement shacks, which are notorious for lethal fires. His concerns go beyond the material: he is committed to helping local children envision themselves in a world transcending their narrow townships. To that end he works with international foundations to create mini "United Nations" associations in local high schools.

To me, Gerald's life seemed exemplary, devoted to uplift and global understanding. Both Billy and I deeply appreciated the time he gave us, the miles he drove that day, and the histories he told. And we understood, or thought we did, his resentments, which he expressed pretty freely as we drove. Despite his clear professional successes, his record of good works, his international contacts, and his apparent financial comfort, his conversations with us brimmed with resentment, not just at the historical injustices of apartheid but at what he sees as continuing discrimination against him and his community. This anger was the second thing that struck us about him. We met Gerald on our second day in the country, so at the time I didn't realize that resentment is a national characteristic. Everyone in South Africa thinks their group is being screwed.

In Gerald's case it was the Jews, which was, of course, where my ears pricked up. Suddenly I was being brought into this lecture. At first I didn't understand why this very courteous man was sounding off against Jews with me sitting next to him. Then I realized that I was the chameleon in the car. If Gerald identified Billy as "Colored" (mind you, he never asked), did he then see me as "Colored" too? Who could tell, on the surface? His wife, whom we met briefly, certainly looked white to us, but she wasn't. (Or maybe she was? I didn't ask, either. Maybe I, too, just assumed?) In any case, it was clear that we were not seeing race as South Africans do. Maybe, in South African eyes, my presence with Billy contextualized me as a white-looking "Colored" person. Or maybe Gerald thought we were both white Americans—a group that defaults to Christian, usually Protestant. Or maybe Gerald sensed I was Jewish and didn't care. His comments about Jews sounded familiar to me. Some of what Gerald was saying reflected a traditional, religiously based anti-Semitism probably traceable to his childhood in a Christian missionary enclave. I've encountered this kind of prejudice throughout my life, even among my in-laws: the assumption that (a) all Jews are businessmen and (b) they are successful because they see everyone who isn't Jewish as fair game. Another source of Gerald's resentment stems from the confluence of recent Jewish history with apartheid's social engineering. Under apartheid, fear and resentment were government instruments. For the government to maintain the social distances that apartheid's ideology dictated, it was useful to convince every South African community that other groups were threatening them: physically, financially, religiously, geographically, racially. It's the old divide-and-conquer strategy.

Moreover, in South Africa, Jews and "Colored" competed in the same territory, in business and the professions. But the Jews had the advantage. The apartheid government classified Jews as whites, which meant they were free to share in the spoils of privilege in South Africa. And on the whole, they did. Even though the antiapartheid movement contained a disproportionate number of activist Jews—heroes and martyrs of the movement like Helen Suzman and Joe Slovo—the bulk of the community turned inward, focusing on internal Jewish affairs rather than national politics. Grateful, after Hitler's Germany, to be classified as "white" but also keenly aware of their historical marginality, the majority of South African Jews succumbed to the paranoia of white fear. As educated and ambitious as the "Colored" population, rather than join hands to confront the power structure, they competed with the "Colored" community for power, recognition, and economic stability. Moreover, despite the recent history of Hitler's Germany, South Africa's Jewish establishment tacitly collaborated with South Africa's neo-Nazi government. That was the face of the Jewish community that people like Gerald saw, not the Jewish activists who fought, were imprisoned, and died in freedom's cause. Driving us around Stellenbosch, Gerald noted bitterly that Jews' obsession with the Holocaust didn't prevent them from exploiting other South Africans, especially black and "Colored."

I didn't cringe during Gerald's lecture; I listened. I told myself that he was talking about South African Jews, not Americans. It wasn't personal, so I should take my notes and keep my mouth shut. The cringe came during our next South Africa encounter. Just before we left the United States, my cousin Rebecca told me that I had relatives in South Africa. The news came as a total surprise. As I had understood my father's family history, half the family came to the United States at the turn of the twentieth century, and the other half stayed in Latvia, where the Nazis eventually wiped them out. Now Rebecca was telling me that some of my grandparents' many siblings had migrated to South Africa when Grandma and Grandpa migrated to New England. That there was a whole branch of the family tree in Durban. She was in touch with them. Did I want her to tell them I was coming?

I said yes.

They called us when we were still in Cape Town, inviting us to Friday night dinner when we got to Durban. Our taxi took us to an apartment complex where, coincidentally, we had spent the afternoon talking with three literature professors from the University of KwaZulu-Natal, all of whom were quick, articulate, informed, and progressive. The relatives, my journal reminds me, gave me another side of South Africa. "You can't spend all your time with guides and the intelligentsia and say that you know or even have lightly surveyed a country," I scolded myself that evening. "These people [i.e., my relatives and their friends] are very much a part of your project."

Definitely a part of the project, and so far the most painful one. It

was easy to listen to South Africans complain about the apartheid government oppressing them; that didn't have anything to do with me,
and besides, I told myself smugly, I'd boycotted South African goods for
years. The Durban cousins *did* have to do with me, because even though
I didn't know them, they were my people. I felt trapped in a net of conflicting emotions: pleasure, gratitude, curiosity, dread, shame. It wasn't
an easy evening, even though my cousins went out of their way to welcome us. Despite having just returned from London, they arranged a dinner party for us. Their friends were warm and welcoming, and the food
was prepared with my vegetarianism in mind. They couldn't have been
kinder or more gracious. It was like going home.

And that was the problem. I was back in Baltimore in 1958.

"Obama was raised as a Muslim," one of the guests opined. "That's
why he is so hostile to Israel."

"The blacks feel entitled," my cousin told us later. "Every year we are
sure they are going to push us into the sea, but so far it hasn't happened."

This was the tenor of the talk, in the rare instances when it wasn't
about daily life, children, and the synagogue. Our host's comment about
the whites being pushed into the sea was telling, I thought; the entire
group spends a lot of time in Israel, and they fused Israeli/Palestinian
conflicts there with white/black conflicts in South Africa. (When we
toured the Apartheid Museum two weeks later I realized just how much
Israel had learned from apartheid; in my mind now there is a very clear
line from Nazi Germany to apartheid South Africa to current-day Israel.)
We sat there listening that night in Durban, while the company talked in
the dining room and the black maid washed dishes in the kitchen.

And no one noticed that Billy was not white.

I think. Or maybe they noticed and didn't care. But I think they
didn't notice, and that they didn't notice because he was with me; we
were an old married couple, and they knew I was Jewish and assumed
he was, too. It was the chameleon effect again. In this house, I was the
landscape into which Billy blended.

When we discussed the evening back in our hotel room, Billy and I
realized that our experiences of South Africa were shaped through frameworks we brought from our American lives. We both came from marginal groups that clung to their proximity to the white power structure.
Billy's distrust of South Africa's "Colored" population fused American
institutions with South African ones, much as my relatives fused Israeli/
Palestinian conflicts with white/black South African ones. My own flight
from 1950s Baltimore racism, as filtered by my Jewish community there,

made me hypersensitive to any sign of Jewish racism. Neither of us could tell how South Africans were reading us, which meant that in this country, we did not know who we were. In South Africa, as Twain divined, little is what it looks to be.

Not all chameleons change color. Maybe the chameleon in Twain's Durban hotel was one of the ones that doesn't. In any case, he describes everything about the chameleon *except* its color changes—and then abruptly switches to other observations about his new environment. The omission seems consonant with his whole approach to South Africa, as if he was willing himself not to probe the enigmas he perceived.

I started this chapter with Uncle Leonard prancing around the living room in his wife's underclothes. Let me briefly come back to him. I notice that I used the term "didn't know" four times in the last two sentences of the anecdote. What did Leonard's act signify? Was he a transvestite? Was he imitating Milton Berle, whose cross-dressing antics convulsed America in the 1950s? Why underwear and jewelry but not a dress? Did the dress signal an interface between the "real," as signaled by the underwear, and the "apparent," as signaled by the accessories? Was he trying to unmask his wife's respectability by juxtaposing hat, gloves, jewelry to girdle, bra, slip? I don't know. I'm not sure anyone in the room knew, including Len himself. So we laughed, just as Olivier Py says his audiences do during his drag shows. And in our laughter, perhaps, there was the dawning recognition that Len might have been telling us something we needed to know: about appearance and reality, about gender fluidity, and about our ability to imagine new identities.

Coda

The Zulu word for greeting is *sawubona*. Its root, *bona*, means "to see." Thus *sawubona* means "I see you." I love it as a greeting because it forces me to confront my habitual New York practice of plunging into my concerns before acknowledging that I'm talking to a real human being. "Sawubona," I learned to say to the hotel clerk in Johannesburg, and she would respond, looking me in the eye, "Ngikhona" (I am here). Then we would get down to business.

Notes

Introduction

1. Throughout this book all quotations from *Following the Equator* refer to the Dover paperback edition, which is abbreviated *FE*.

2. Please note: I have eschewed use of the preferred term "Aboriginal and Torres Strait Peoples" for the remainder of this book because it was not used during Twain's era.

3. I should note that the book was published in two different editions: *Following the Equator* for the US audience, and *More Tramps Abroad* for the British—both first published in 1897.

4. Twain, Livy, and Clara almost circled the globe. Returning to the United States from England, where they had been living, they sojourned in Elmira while Twain put together drafts of his lectures, and then they "test-drove" the lectures on a tour through the upper Midwest and Canada before embarking for Australia from Vancouver. Their return to London from South Africa thirteen months later completed their near circuit of the world.

Chapter 1

1. The Henry W. and Albert A. Berg Collection of English and American Literature at the New York Public Library, Forty-Second Street branch, has letters from Twain to Chatto and Windus written during the winter of 1896–1897. Several request books that he needed for background while writing *FE*, and some of these, such as Olive Schreiner's *Story of an African Farm*, are directly referenced in *FE*. Twain also requested books from the Chelsea Library near him in London, such as William Knighton's *Private Life of an Eastern King*. See David H. Frears, *Mark Twain Day-by-Day: An Annotated Chronology of the Life of Samuel L. Clemens*, vol. 2, *1886–1896* (Banks, OR: Horizon Micro Publishers), 1104.

2. Twain's bankruptcy was the result of both the failure of his publishing company, Charles L. Webster and Company, and his investment in the Paige typesetting machine. He entered bankruptcy proceedings in 1894 and settled his debts (paying one hundred cents on the dollar owed) by 1898. Henry B. Wonham and Lawrence Howe's recent *Mark Twain and Money: Language, Capital, and Culture* (Tuscaloosa: University of Alabama Press, 2017) contains several excellent essays focused on the bankruptcy, its causes, and its aftermath.

3. Benares/Varanasi has had numerous names, among which three—Kashi, Benares, and Varanasi—have been the best known. Dr. Rana Singh notes that Kashi, which means "concentration of cosmic light," is the oldest of the names, going back to 1500 BCE. "Varanasi" was used to denote the city in the Puranic period (200 BCE to 1100 CE, though this temporal swath is also divided into three subsections: Epic, Early, and Classical), as the city lying

between the Varana and Asi Rivers. Buddhists referred to the city as Banarasi or Banaras, and the British adopted that name, spelling it variously Benares, Bunarus, Banaras, or Benaras. In 1956 the Indian government declared that "Varanasi" would henceforth be the official name. See Rana P. B. Singh and Pravin S. Rana, *Banaras Region: A Spiritual and Cultural Guide* (Varanasi, India: Indica Books, 2006), 28–30.

4. For a sampling of recent discussions of Twain and faith, see especially William E. Phipps, *Mark Twain's Religion* (Macon, GA: Mercer University Press, 2003), Joe B. Fulton, *The Reverend Mark Twain: Theological Burlesque, Form, and Content* (Columbus: Ohio State University Press, 2006), Harold K. Bush Jr., *Mark Twain and the Spiritual Crisis of His Age* (Tuscaloosa: University of Alabama Press, 2007), and Peter Messent, *Mark Twain and Male Friendship: The Twichell, Howells, & Rogers Friendships* (New York: Oxford University Press, 2009).

5. All references to *A Connecticut Yankee in King Arthur's Court* refer to the University of California edition.

6. For an excellent bibliography on the discovery of germ theory and its implications for public health, see Harvard University's online website Contagion: Historical Views of Diseases and Epidemics, http://ocp.hul.harvard.edu/contagion/germtheory.html. How people understand the origins and spread of disease is central to public health initiatives, and these understandings vary greatly according to time, region, religion, and prevailing metaphysics.

7. The hymn, written in 1819, was so popular that it is worth reprinting here, courtesy of Hymnal.net, https://www.hymnal.net/en/hymn/h/915.

> From Greenland's icy mountains, from India's coral strand;
> Where Afric's sunny fountains roll down their golden sand:
> From many an ancient river, from many a palmy plain,
> They call us to deliver their land from error's chain.
>
> What though the spicy breezes blow soft o'er Ceylon's isle;
> Though every prospect pleases, and only man is vile?
> In vain with lavish kindness the gifts of God are strown;
> The heathen in his blindness bows down to wood and stone.
>
> Shall we, whose souls are lighted with wisdom from on high,
> Shall we to those benighted the lamp of life deny?
> Salvation! O salvation! The joyful sound proclaim,
> Till earth's remotest nation has learned Messiah's Name.
>
> Waft, waft, ye winds, His story, and you, ye waters, roll
> Till, like a sea of glory, it spreads from pole to pole:
> Till o'er our ransomed nature the Lamb for sinners slain,
> Redeemer, King, Creator, in bliss returns to reign.

8. David Frears notes that in January 1896, while on the boat from Australia

to India, Twain copied Heber's missionary hymn into his notebook (vol. 2, 1099). The "only man is vile" line appears in Twain's 1901 notes for "Second Advent," one of his furious outbursts about American foreign policy at the onset of the twentieth century: "Second Advent. Begins triumphal march around the globe at Tien Tsin . . . preceded by Generals, Warships, cavalry, infantry, artillery, who clear the road & pile the dead & the loot . . . for 'propagation of the Gospel,' . . . singing 'where every prospect pleases & only man is vile.' Christ arrives in a vast war-fleet furnished by the Great Powers." See Notebook 44, 1901, p. 20, Mark Twain Papers, Berkeley, California.

9. For an in-depth review of this history, see Nicholas Dirks, *The Scandal of Empire: India and the Creation of Imperial Britain* (Cambridge, MA: Harvard University Press, 2006).

10. Mary Boewe has also tackled this issue, in an online article titled "How Mark Twain Found God in India," Academia, 2018, http://www.academia.edu/1472306/How_Mark_Twain_Found_God_in_India.

Chapter 2

1. Twain refers to this scientist as "Mr. Henkin." In fact he was E. H. Hankin, one of the early investigators into the existence of bacteriophages. See "Wikipedia: Ernest Hanbury Hankin," Wikimedia Foundation, last modified April 24, 2019, https://en.wikipedia.org/wiki/Ernest_Hanbury_Hankin.

2. Mark Twain Letters, #36, February 27, 1896. Courtesy of the Mark Twain Project, University of California, Berkeley.

3. "Pollutants in Ganga Destroying River Purifying Algae Colonies," *Hindustan Times*, May 16, 2017, https://www.hindustantimes.com/lucknow/pollutants-in-ganga-destroying-river-purifying-algae-colonies-study/story-2B1KIr59n07j5PeAasDmSK.html.

4. Suprita Anupan, "Why Do People Litter in India? Lack of Individual Social Responsibility," *Clean India Journal*, July 23, 2014, https://www.cleanindiajournal.com/%E2%80%98why-do-people-litter-in-india%E2%80%99lack-of-individual-social-responsibility/.

5. Vasant Natarajan, "Why Are We Such Litterbugs?," *The Hindu*, July 28, 2013, https://www.thehindu.com/todays-paper/tp-features/tp-openpage/why-are-we-such-litterbug/article4962158.ece.

6. Sonal Kalra, "Swachh Bharat: C'Mon, It's Time to Come Clean," A Calmer You Column, October 5, 2014, http://www.sonalkalra.com/swachh-bharat-cmon-time-come-clean/.

7. Saurabh Daga, "What Makes Us (Indians) Disgracefully Shameless to Litter on Roads and Other Public Places?," *Quora*, August 18, 2014, https://www.quora.com/What-makes-us-Indians-disgracefully-shameless-to-litter-on-roads-and-other-public-places.

Chapter 3

1. *The Last Rites of the Honourable Mr. Rai*, by Jayasinhji Jhala, Laurent Sem-

mel, and Alethea Carbaus, originally produced by Documentary Educational Resources, Watertown, MA, 2007; currently produced by Kanopy Streaming, San Francisco, CA, 2014. The video was made at the request of the family. I discovered it in searches for "Varanasi" and "cremation" in the KU libraries.

2. Mark Twain, *Roughing It*, Signet ed. (New York: New American Library, 1962).

Chapter 4

1. *For the Term of His Natural Life* has a complicated publication history. It was originally serialized under the title *His Natural Life* in the *Australian Journal* in 1870–1872 and then published under the same name in Australia by George Robertson in 1874 and in London by Richard Bentley & Sons in 1875. Bentley republished the novel under the title *For the Term of His Natural Life* in 1882, a year after Clarke's death. The Mark Twain Papers holds a copy from *The Austral Edition of the Selected Works of Marcus Clarke* (Melbourne: Fergusson & Mitchell, 1890), which has Twain's markings. It is currently available from multiple publishers.

2. Popularly dated 1816 and known as "Governor Davey's Proclamation Board," the Board was actually produced in 1829 under the administration of Governor Sir George Arthur. In *FE*, Twain refers to it only as "Governor's Proclamation Board." See Kerry Driscoll, *Mark Twain among the Indians and Other Indigenous Peoples* (Oakland: University of California Press, 2018), 298–300.

3. S. L. Clemens, *Following the Equator*, undated typescript, 287–88 (fifty-six additional pages of the typescript were not used in the published work), Henry W. and Albert A. Berg Collection of English and American Literature, New York Public Library. I also thank the Mark Twain Foundation, which owns the copyright to Mark Twain's work.

4. Of course the degree and extent of interethnic violence during the colonial period is subject to dispute in Australia, as in other countries. For a much fuller sense of the historiography of settler and Aborigine relations, see the work of historians Henry Reynolds and Keith Windschuttle, who argue from opposite sides. See especially Henry Reynolds and C. D. Rowley, *The Other Side of the Frontier: Aborigine Resistance to the European Invasion of Australia* (Melbourne: Penguin Books Australia, 1990); and Keith Windschuttle, *The Fabrication of Aborigine History*, vol. 1, *Van Diemen's Land 1803–1847* (Paddington, Australia: Macleay Press, 2004).

5. Chris Buckley, "China Is Detaining Muslims in Vast Numbers. The Goal: 'Transformation,'" *New York Times*, September 9, 2018, https://thenewdaily.com.au/news/world/2018/09/09/china-uighur-muslims/.

Chapter 5

1. Dwayne Eutsey, "'Beyond the Devil's Race-Track and the Everlasting Sunday': John Tuckey, Transcendence, and Mark Twain's #44, *The Mysterious Stranger*" (unpublished paper delivered at the Eighth International Conference

on the State of Mark Twain Studies, Elmira College, August 3–5, 2017). My thanks to Mr. Eutsey for providing me with a copy of this paper.

2. "Understanding Aboriginal Dreamings," Artlandish Aborigine Art Gallery, https://www.aboriginal-art-australia.com/aboriginal-art-library/understanding-aboriginal-dreaming-and-the-dreamtime/.

3. Cathy Craigie, private correspondence with the author, May 25, 2016. My warmest thanks to Cathy Craigie, whose willingness to talk and correspond with me has been invaluable.

4. Cathy Craigie, private correspondence with the author.

Chapter 6

1. Not to be confused with the Taronga Zoo Sydney, operated by the Zoological Parks Board of New South Wales.

2. Indeed, the *New York Times* featured a story about an Idaho fish and game commissioner whose lurid pictures of animals he had killed on an African game farm drew so much criticism that he was forced to resign. Matt Stevens and Sarah Mervosh, "Idaho Fish and Game Commissioner Resigns amid Criticism over African Hunting Photos," *New York Times*, October 15, 2018.

3. Mark Twain's unpublished journals, May 30–31, 1896, Mark Twain Project, Berkeley, California. I also thank the Mark Twain Foundation, which owns the copyright to all of Mark Twain's writings.

4. Clemens first saw a Church painting in 1861, when Church's *Heart of the Andes* was exhibited at the Western Academy of Art in St. Louis. He went back to view it three times and described it in a letter to his brother Orion in glowing terms. (Samuel L. Clemens to Orion Clemens, March 18, 1861, in *Mark Twain's Letters*, vol. 1, *1853–1866*, 117.) The writer and the painter became friends thirty years later. The Mark Twain Project holds at least three as yet unpublished letters from Church to Clemens, all written in the late 1880s and early 1890s. "Letters," Mark Twain Project Online, University of California, Berkeley.

5. The Bass Strait is the 160-mile-wide channel between the island of Tasmania and the Australian continent, connecting the Tasman Sea and the Indian Ocean.

6. My thanks to research manager Dann for speaking with me.

7. "Rotorua Hangi Dinner and Performance," Viator, https://www.viator.com/tours/Rotorua/Rotorua-Maori-Hangi-Dinner-and-Performance/d395-2295HANGI.

Chapter 7

1. To Jane Lampton Clemens, August 24, 1853, *Mark Twain's Letters*, vol. 1, *1853–1866*, 4.

2. "Wikipedia: James Rose Innes," Wikimedia Foundation, last modified December 14, 2018, https://en.wikipedia.org/wiki/James_Rose_Innes.

3. "Twain Likes the Vaal. Praises South Africa and Prophesies a Great Future," *Chicago Daily Tribune*, August 1, 1896, 3.

4. "Cecil Rhodes as a Woman Hater," *Wanganui Herald* (New Zealand), May 14, 1902, https://paperspast.natlib.govt.nz/newspapers/WH19020514.2.6.

Bibliography

Works by Mark Twain

Autobiography of Mark Twain, The, Vol. 3. Edited by Benjamin Griffin and Harriet Elinor Smith. Berkeley, CA: University of California Press, 2015.

Following the Equator: A Journey around the World. New York: Dover, 1989. Unaltered republication of the 1st ed., Hartford, CT: American Publishing, 1897.

Mark Twain: Collected Tales, Sketches, Speeches, & Essays. Vol. 1, *1852–1890.* Vol. 2, *1891–1910.* Edited by Louis J. Budd. New York: Library of America, 1992.

Mark Twain: The Mysterious Stranger Manuscripts. Edited by William M. Gibson. Berkeley: University of California Press, 1969.

Mark Twain's Correspondence with Henry Huttleston Rogers, 1893–1909. Edited by Louis Leary. Berkeley: University of California Press, 1969.

Mark Twain's Letters. Vol. 1, *1853–1866.* Edited by Edgar Marquess Branch, Michael Barry Frank, Kenneth M. Sanderson, Harriet E. Smith, Lin Salamo, and Richard Bucci. Berkeley: University of California Press, 1988.

Mark Twain's Satires and Burlesques. Edited by Franklin Rogers. Berkeley: University of California Press, 1968.

Roughing It. Signet ed. New York: New American Library, 1962.

Other Works Cited, Referenced, or Consulted

Adams, Sir John. *Everyman's Psychology.* New York: Doubleday, Doran, 1929.

Alley, Kelley D. *On the Banks of the Ganges: When Wastewater Meets Sacred Water.* Ann Arbor: University of Michigan Press, 2002.

Baror, Shira, and Moshe Bar. "Associative Activation and Its Relation to Exploration and Exploitation in the Brain." *Psychological Science* 27, no. 6 (2016): 776–89.

Berger, John. "Why Look at Animals?" In *About Looking*, 3–28. New York: Pantheon Books, 1980.

Berndt, Ronald Murray. *Australian Aboriginal Religion.* Fascicle 1, *Introduction: The South-Eastern Region.* Leiden, Netherlands: E. J. Brill, 1974.

Bird, John. "Dreams and Metaphors in *No. 44, The Mysterious Stranger.*" In *Centenary Reflections on Mark Twain's "No. 44, The Mysterious Stranger,"* edited by Joseph Csicsila and Chad Rohman, 198–215. Columbia: University of Missouri Press, 2009.

Bonwick, James. *Daily Life and Origin of the Tasmanians.* London: Sampson, Low, Son, and Marston, 1870.

———. *The Last of the Tasmanians; or, The Black War of Van Dieman's Land.* London: Sampson Low, Son, and Marston, 1870.

Bridgman, Richard. *Traveling in Mark Twain*. Berkeley: University of California Press, 1987.

"Cecil Rhodes as a Woman Hater." *Wanganui Herald* (New Zealand), May 14, 1902. https://paperspast.natlib.govt.nz/newspapers/WH19020514.2.6.

Chanishvili, Nina. "Experience of the Eliava Institute of Bacteriophage, Microbiology and Virology in Development of the Innovative Bio-Preparations and Their Commercialization." Innovative Drug Discovery Workshop, ISTC, Toronto, Canada, August 6–10, 2011. Tbilisi, Georgia: Eliava Institute of Bacteriophages, Microbiology and Virology. http://data.istc.int/ISTC/ISTC.nsf/va_WebResources/News_Drug_Design&Development/$-file/Chanishvili_Nina.pdf.

Chapin, Adèle Le Bourgeois. *Their Trackless Way: A Book of Memories*. Edited by Christine Chapin. New York: H. Holt, 1932.

Charlesworth, Max. Introduction to *Aboriginal Religions in Australia: An Anthology of Recent Writings*, edited by Max Charlesworth, Francoise Dussart, and Howard Morphy, 1–27. Aldershot, UK: Ashgate, 2005.

Chatwin, Bruce. *The Songlines*. New York: Viking Press, 1987.

Clarke, Marcus. *For the Term of His Natural Life*. Teddington, UK: Echo Library, 2007.

Cleversley, Keith. "Entoptic Imagery and Altered States of Consciousness." Entheology.com: Preserving Shamanism's Ancient Sacred Knowledge. October 2012. http://entheology.com/research/entoptic-imagery-and-altered-states-of-consciousness/.

Competition Tribunal of South Africa. Case No. 100/LM/Sep07. Business Venture Investments No. 1145 (PTY) LTD and Nkomazi Wilderness. November 7, 2007.

———. Case No. 100/LM/Sep07. Business Venture Investments No. 1145 (PTY) LTD and Nkomazi Wilderness. ZACT 86. November 8, 2007.

———. Dubai World Africa Conservation FZE Business Venture Investments No. 1145 (PTY) Ltd (41/LM/Apr08) [2008] ZACT 51. July 8, 2008.

Conway, Moncure D. *My Pilgrimage to the Wise Men of the East*. Boston: Houghton Mifflin, 1906.

Cooper, Robert. *Around the World with Mark Twain*. New York: Arcade, 2000.

Dalby, Simon. "Framing the Anthropocene: The Good, the Bad, and the Ugly." *Anthropocene Review* 3, no. 1: 33–51.

Das, Priyam, and Kenneth R. Tamminga. "The Ganges and the GAP: Assessing the Efforts to Clean a Sacred River." *Sustainability* 4 (2012): 1647–68.

Dirks, Nicholas B. *The Scandal of Empire: India and the Creation of Imperial Britain*. Cambridge, MA: Harvard University Press, 2006.

Dodson, Michael S., ed. *Banaras: Urban Forms and Cultural Histories*. New York: Routledge, 2012.

Dolmetsch, Carl. *"Our Famous Guest": Mark Twain in Vienna*. Athens: University of Georgia Press, 1992.

Driscoll, Kerry. *Mark Twain among the Indians and Other Indigenous Peoples.* Oakland: University of California Press, 2018.

Eck, Diana L. *Banares, City of Light.* New York: Columbia University Press, 1999.

———. *Darśan: Seeing the Divine Image in India.* 2nd ed. New York: Columbia University Press, 1996.

Eliade, Mircea. *Australian Religions: An Introduction.* Ithaca: Cornell University Press, 1973.

Eutsey, Dwayne. "Waking from this Dream of Separateness: Hinduism and the Ending of *No. 44, The Mysterious Stranger.*" *Mark Twain Annual* 7, no. 1 (2009): 66–77.

Fishkin, Shelley Fisher. *Mark Twain's Book of Animals.* Berkeley: University of California Press, 2010.

Frears, David H. *Mark Twain Day-by-Day: An Annotated Chronology of the Life of Samuel L. Clemens.* Vol. 2, *1886–1896.* Vol. 3, *1897–1904.* Banks, OR: Horizon Micro Publishers, 2011.

Freitag, Sandria B., ed. *Culture and Power in Banaras: Community, Performance, and Environment, 1800–1980.* Berkeley: University of California Press, 1989.

Garber, Marjorie. *Vested Interests: Cross-Dressing and Cultural Anxiety.* New York: Routledge, 1992.

Gaynes, Robert P. *Germ Theory: Medical Pioneers in Infectious Diseases.* Washington, DC: ASM Press, 2011.

Gold, Charles H. *"Hatching Ruin": or Mark Twain's Road to Bankruptcy.* Columbia: University of Missouri Press, 2003.

Gómez, Miguel Andrea ("Gol"). *A Pilgrimage to Kashi: History, Mythology and Culture of the Strangest and Most Fascinating City in India.* Varanasi, India: Indica Books, 1999.

Gormer, James. "Plan to Export Chimps Tests Law to Protect Species." *New York Times,* November 16, 2015.

Gribben, Alan. *Mark Twain's Library: A Reconstruction.* 2 vols. Boston: G. K. Hall, 1980.

Haberman, David L. *River of Love in an Age of Pollution: The Yamuna River of Northern India.* Berkeley: University of California Press, 2006.

Hacking, Ian. *Historical Ontology.* Cambridge, MA: Harvard University Press, 2002.

Han, Erze, and Joseph O'Mahoney. "The British Colonial Origins of Anti-Gay Laws." Monkey Cage, *Washington Post,* October 30, 2014.

Harris, Gardiner. "Falcon Hunters Become Fervent Preservationists." *New York Times,* January 4, 2015.

———. "Poor Sanitation in India May Afflict Well-Fed Children with Malnutrition." *New York Times,* July 13, 2014.http://www.nytimes.com/2014/07/15/world/asia/

poor-sanitation-in-india-may-afflict-well-fed-children-with-malnutrition. html?_r=0.

Hart, Dr. Ernest, F. R. C. S. "The Pilgrim Path of Cholera." *Popular Science Monthly* 43 (October 1893): 634–51.

Havell, E. B. *Benares: The Sacred City; Sketches of Hindu Life and Religion.* London: Blackie and Son, 1905.

Herman, Daniel Justin. *Hunting and the American Imagination.* Washington, DC: Smithsonian Institution Press, 2001.

Hertel, Bradley R., and Cynthia Ann Humes, eds. *Living Banares: Hindu Religion in Cultural Context.* Albany, NY: SUNY Press, 1993.

Hollander, Anne. *Seeing through Clothes.* New York: Viking Press, 1978.

Hume, Lynne. *Ancestral Power: The Dreaming, Consciousness, and Aboriginal Australians.* Melbourne: Melbourne University Press, 2002.

Jacoby, Karl. *Crimes against Nature: Squatters, Poachers, Thieves, and the Hidden History of American Conservation.* Berkeley: University of California Press, 2001.

Jones, Karen R. *Epiphany in the Wilderness: Hunting, Nature, and Performance in the Nineteenth-Century American West.* Boulder: University Press of Colorado, 2015.

Khilnani, Sunil. *The Idea of India.* New Delhi: Penguin Books, 1998.

Knoper, Randall. "'Silly Creations of an Imagination That Is Not Conscious of Its Freaks': Multiple Selves, Wordless Communication, and the Psychology of Mark Twain's *No. 44, The Mysterious Stranger.*" In *Centenary Reflections on Mark Twain's "No. 44, The Mysterious Stranger,"* edited by Joseph Csicsila and Chad Rohman, 144–156. Columbia: University of Missouri Press, 2009.

Lavigne, David, Rosamund Kidman Cox, Vivek Menon, and Michael Wamithi. "Reinventing Wildlife Conservation for the 21st Century." In *Gaining Ground: In Pursuit of Ecological Sustainability,* edited by David M. Lavigne and Sheryl Fink, 379–406. Guelph, ON: IFAW (International Fund for Animal Welfare), 2006.

Lochtefeld, James. *God's Gateway: Identity and Meaning in a Hindu Pilgrimage Place.* New York: Oxford University Press, 2009.

Lorimer, Jamie. *Wildlife in the Anthropocene: Conservation after Nature.* Minneapolis: University of Minnesota Press, 2015.

———. "Wildlife in the Anthropocene: Environmentalism without Nature." University of Oxford Podcasts. October 2, 2014. Podcasts.ox.ac.uk/ wildlife-anthropocene-environmentalism-without-nature.

Macfarlane, Robert. "Generation Anthropocene: How Humans Have Altered the Planet Forever." *The Guardian,* April 1, 2016.

Menon, Vivek, and David Lavigne. "Attitudes, Values, and Objectives: The Real Basis of Wildlife Conservation." In *Gaining Ground: In Pursuit of Ecological Sustainability,* edited by David M. Lavigne and Sheryl Fink,

173–89. Guelph, ON: IFAW (International Fund for Animal Welfare), 2006.

Merry, Kay. "The Cross-Cultural Relationships between the Sealers and the Tasmanian Aboriginal Women at Bass Strait and Kangaroo Island in the Early Nineteenth Century." *Counterpoints* (2003): 80–88. http://ehlt. flinders.edu.au/projects/counterpoints/Proc_2003/A8.pdf.

Messent, Peter. *Mark Twain and Male Friendship: The Twichell, Howells, & Rogers Friendships.* New York: Oxford University Press, 2009.

———. "Racial and Colonial Discourse in Mark Twain's *Following the Equator.*" *Essays in Arts and Sciences* 22 (October 1993): 67–83.

Michel, Mark A., ed. *Preserving Wildlife: An International Perspective.* Amherst, NY: Humanity Books, 1999.

Michelson, Bruce. "Mark Twain's Mysterious Strangers and the Motions of the Mind." In *Centenary Reflections on Mark Twain's "No. 44, The Mysterious Stranger,"* edited by Joseph Csicsila and Chad Rohman, 216–35. Columbia: University of Missouri Press, 2009.

Mielke, Laura L. *Moving Encounters: Sympathy and the Indian Question in Antebellum Literature.* Amherst: University of Massachusetts Press, 2008.

Mills, James H., and Satadru Sen, eds. *Confronting the Body: The Politics of Physicality in Colonial and Post-Colonial India.* London: Anthem Press, 2004.

Mohanty, Sachidananda, ed. *Travel Writing and the Empire.* New Delhi: KATHA, 2003.

Morgan, Henry Lewis. *Ancient Society: Or, Researches in the Lines of Human Progress from Savagery, through Barbarism to Civilization.* New York: Henry Holt, 1877.

Morinis, E. Alan. *Pilgrimage in the Hindu Tradition: A Case Study of West Bengal.* Delhi: Oxford University Press, 1984.

Morris, Linda A. *Gender Play in Mark Twain: Cross-Dressing and Transgression.* Columbia: University of Missouri Press, 2007.

Mountford, Charles P. *The Dreamtime: Australian Aboriginal Myths in Paintings by Ainslie Roberts with Text by Charles P. Mountford.* Adelaide, South Australia: Rigby, 1965.

Mutalik, Keshav. *Mark Twain in India.* Bombay, India: Noble Publishing House, 1978.

Nath, Vijay. *Dynamics of the Ritual Gift System: Some Unexplored Dimensions.* New Delhi: Manohar Publishers, 2012.

Parker, Arthur. *Guide to Benares.* Benares, India: E. J. Lazarus, 1895.

Parker, Janet, and Julie Stanton, eds. *Mythology: Myths, Legends, and Fantasies.* Cape Town: Struik Publishers, 2007.

Parkman, Francis. *The Jesuits in North America in the 17th Century.* Boston: Little, Brown, 1894.

Parry, Jonathan P. *Death in Banares.* Cambridge: Cambridge University Press, 1994.

Pérez-Peña, Richard. "Report Says Census Undercounts Mixed Race." *New York Times*, June 12, 2015.

Philippon, Daniel L. "Mark Twain in South Africa, Day by Day." *Mark Twain Journal* 40, no. 1 (Spring 2002): 14–24.

Plomley, N. J. B., ed. *Friendly Mission: The Tasmanian Journals and Papers of George Augustus Robinson, 1829–1834*. Hobart, Tasmania: Tasmanian Historical Research Association, 1966.

Poirier, Sylvia. "This Is Good Country. We Are Good Dreamers." In *Dream Travelers: Sleep Experiences and Culture in the Western Pacific*, edited by Roger Ivar Lohmann, 107–25. New York: Palgrave Macmillan, 2003.

Regan, Sheila. "In Mainstream Museums, Confronting Colonialism while Curating Native American Art." *Hyperallergic*, June 26, 2015, 1–6.

Reiger, John F. *American Sportsmen and the Origins of Conservation*. New York: Winchester Press, 1975.

Rogers, Guy. "Top Award Makes It 10 in Row for Shamwari." *Herald Online*, January 8, 2008. https://www.worldtravelawards.com/news-189.

Scheuering, Rachel White. *Shapers of the Great Debate on Conservation: A Biographical Dictionary*. Westport, CT: Greenwood Press, 2004.

Schillingsburg, Miriam Jones. *At Home Abroad: Mark Twain in Australasia*. Jackson: University Press of Mississippi, 1988.

Sevier, Laura. "The Wild Life of Adrian Gardiner." Mantis Collection. Interview, June 27, 2012. http://www.mantiscollection.com/wild-life-adrian-gardiner/.

Singh, Rana P. B., and Pravin S. Rana. *Banaras Region: A Spiritual and Cultural Guide*. Varanasi, India: Indica Books, 2006.

Sleeman, W. H. *Rambles and Recollections of an Indian Official, by Lieutenant-Colonel W. H. Sleeman*. 2 vols. London: J. Hatchard & Son, 1844.

Smith, David Lionel. "Samuel Clemens, Duality, and Time Travel." In *Centenary Reflections on Mark Twain's "No. 44, The Mysterious Stranger,"* edited by Joseph Csicsila and Chad Rohman, 187–97. Columbia: University of Missouri Press, 2009.

Smyth, R. Brough. *The Aborigines of Victoria: With Notes Relating to the Habits of the Natives of Other Parts of Australia and Tasmania*. London: John Ferres, 1878.

Stone, Richard. "Stalin's Forgotten Cure." *Science* 298, no. 5594 (October 25, 2002): 728–31. http://science.sciencemag.org/content/298/5594/728.

Strathcarron, Ian. *The Indian Equator: Mark Twain's India Revisited*. Mineola, NY: Dover, 2013.

Tomalin, Emma. "Bio-Divinity and Biodiversity: Perspectives on Religion and Environmental Conservation in India." *Numen* 51, no. 3 (2004): 265–95. http://www.jstor.org/stable/3270584.

Turner, Robin L. "Communities, Wildlife Conservation, and Tourism-Based Development: Can Community-Based Nature Tourism Live Up to Its

Promise?" *Journal of International Wildlife Law and Policy* 7 (2004): 161–82.

"Understanding Aboriginal Dreamings." Artlandish Aboriginal Art Gallery. https://www.aboriginal-art-australia.com/aboriginal-art-library/understanding-aboriginal-dreaming-and-the-dreamtime/.

US Department of State. *Papers Relating to the Foreign Relations of the United States. General Index to the Published Volumes of the Diplomatic Correspondence and Foreign Relations of the United States, 1861–1899.* Washington, DC: Government Printing Office, 1902. [Note: the materials referencing Robert Chapin appear on p. 405 in both this and *Money and Prices in Foreign Countries*, below.]

US Department of State, Bureau of Statistics. Special Consular Reports. *Money and Prices in Foreign Countries, Being a Series of Reports upon the Currency Systems of Various Nations in Their Relation to Prices of Commodities and Wages of Labor.* Vol. 13, Part 1. 54th Congress, Second Session, House of Representatives Document No. 25. Washington, DC: Government Printing Office, 1896. [Note: the materials referencing Robert Chapin appear on p. 405 in both this and *Papers Relating to the Foreign Relations*, above.]

US Geological Survey. *Phage Therapy for Florida Corals?* US Geological Survey Fact Sheet 2007-3065. August 2007. https://pubs.usgs.gov/fs/2007/3065/pdf/fs2007-3065.pdf.

Watson, Don. *The Wayward Tourist: Mark Twain's Adventures in Australia.* Melbourne: Melbourne University Press, 2006.

Welland, Dennis. *Mark Twain in England.* London: Chatto & Windus, 1978.

Wetzel, Betty. *After You, Mark Twain: A Modern Journey around the Equator.* Golden, CO: Fulcrum Publishing, 1990.

"Wikipedia: James Rose Innes." Wikimedia Foundation. Last modified December 14, 2018. https://en.wikipedia.org/wiki/James_Rose_Innes.

Wonham, Henry B., and Lawrence Howe, eds. *Mark Twain and Money: Language, Capital, and Culture.* Tuscaloosa: University of Alabama Press, 2017.

Zacks, Richard. *Chasing the Last Laugh: Mark Twain's Raucous and Redemptive Round-the-World Comedy Tour.* New York: Doubleday, 2016.

Zaehner, R. C. *Hinduism.* New York: Oxford University Press, 1966.

Videos

First Australians, The. Blackfella Films. Rachel Perkins, director/writer/producer. 2008. Seven Episodes: "They Have Come to Stay," "Her Will to Survive," "Freedom for Our Lifetime," "There Is No Other Law," "Unhealthy Government Experiment," "Strength to Stand a Long Time," "We Are No Longer Shadows." http://www.sbs.com.au/firstaustralians/.

Last Rites of the Honourable Mr. Rai, The. By Jayasinhji Jhala, Laurent Semmel, and Alethea Carbaus. Originally produced by Documentary Educational Resources, Watertown, MA, 2007. Currently produced by Kanopy Streaming, San Francisco, CA, 2014. Video of a cremation on the five-thousand-year-old Harish Chandra Ghat in Varanasi.

Story of India, The. Hosted by British historian Michael Wood. PBS/BBC. 2007. MayaVision International, 2008. Disk 1: "Beginnings," "The Power of Ideas," "Spice Routes and Silk Roads." Disk 2: "Ages of Gold," "The Meeting of Two Oceans," "Freedom."

Index